John Dando Sedding, Edward Francis Russell

Garden-craft old and new

John Dando Sedding, Edward Francis Russell

Garden-craft old and new

ISBN/EAN: 9783337374532

Printed in Europe, USA, Canada, Australia, Japan

Cover: Foto ©Lupo / pixelio.de

More available books at **www.hansebooks.com**

GARDEN-CRAFT

OLD AND NEW

BY THE LATE
JOHN D. SEDDING

WITH MEMORIAL NOTICE BY THE
REV. E. F. RUSSELL

SIXTEEN ILLUSTRATIONS

LONDON
KEGAN PAUL, TRENCH, TRÜBNER & Co., Lᴛᴅ.
PATERNOSTER HOUSE, CHARING CROSS ROAD
1891

PREFACE.

"*What am I to say for my book?*" asks Mr. Stevenson in the Preface to "*An Inland Voyage.*" "*Caleb and Joshua brought back from Palestine a formidable bunch of grapes; alas! my book produces naught so nourishing; and, for the matter of that, we live in an age when people prefer a definition to any quantity of fruit.*"

As this apology is so uncalled for in the case of this fruitful little volume, I would venture to purloin it, and apply it where it is wholly suitable. Here, the critic will say, is an architect who makes gardens for the houses he builds, writing upon his proper craft, pandering to that popular preference for a definition of which Mr. Stevenson speaks, by offering descriptions of what he thinks a fine garden should be, instead of useful figured plans of its beauties!

And yet, to tell truth, it is more my subject than myself that is to blame if my book be unpractical. Once upon a time complete in itself, as a brief treatise upon the technics of gardening delivered to my brethren of the Art-worker's Guild a year ago, the essay had no sooner arrived with me at home, than it fell to pieces, lost gravity and compactness, and became a garden-plaything—a sort of gardener's "open letter," to take *loose pages as fancies occurred.* So have these errant thoughts, jotted down in the broken leisure of a busy life, grown solid unawares and expanded into a would-be-serious contribution to garden-literature.

Following upon the original lines of the Essay on the For and Against of Modern Gardening, I became the more confirmed as to the general rightness of the old ways of applying Art, and of interpreting Nature the more I studied old gardens and the point of view of their makers; until I now appear as advocate of old types of design, which, I am persuaded, are more consonant with the traditions of English life, and more suitable to an English homestead than some now in vogue.

The old-fashioned garden, whatever its failings in the eyes of the modern landscape-gardener (great is the poverty of his invention), represents one of the pleasures of England, one of the charms of that quiet beautiful life of bygone times that I, for one, would fain see revived. And judged even as pieces of handicraft, apart from their poetic interest, these gardens are worthy of careful study. They embody ideas of ancient worth; they evidence fine aims and heroic efforts; they exemplify traditions that are the net result of a long probation. Better still, they render into tangible shapes old moods of mind that English landscape has inspired; they testify to old devotion to the scenery of our native land, and illustrate old attempts to idealise its pleasant traits.

Because the old gardens are what they are—beautiful yesterday, beautiful to-day, and beautiful always—

we do well to turn to them, not to copy their exact lines, nor to limit ourselves to the range of their ornament and effects, but to glean hints for our garden-enterprise to-day, to drink of their spirit, to gain impulsion from them. As often as not, the forgotten field proves the richest of pastures.

J. D. S.

The Croft, West Wickham, Kent,
  Oct. 8, 1890.

MEMOIR.

THE Manuscript of this book was placed complete in the hands of his publishers by John Sedding. He did not live to see its production.

At the wish of his family and friends, I have, with help from others, set down some memories and impressions of my friend.

My acquaintance with John Sedding dates from the year 1875. He was then 37 years of age, and had been practising as an architect almost exclusively in the South-West of England. The foundations of this practice were laid by his equally talented brother, Edmund Sedding, who, like himself, had received his training in the office of Mr. Street. Edmund died in 1868, and John took up the business, but his clients were so few, and the prospect of an increase in their number so little encouraging, that he left Bristol and came to London, and here I first met him. He had just taken a house in Charlotte Street, Bedford Square, and the house served him on starting both for home and office.

The first years in London proved no exception to the rule of first years, they were more or less a time of struggle and anxiety. John Sedding's happy, buoyant nature, his joy in his art, and invincible faith in his mission, did much to carry him through all difficulties. But both at this time, and all through his life, he owed much, very much, to the brave hopefulness and wise love of his wife.

Rose Sedding, a daughter of Canon Tinling, of Gloucester, lives in the memory of those who knew her as an impersonation of singular spiritual beauty and sweetness. Gentle and refined, sensitive and sympathetic to an unusual degree, there was no lack in her of the sterner stuff of character—force, courage, and endurance. John Sedding leaned upon his wife; indeed, I cannot think of him without her, or guess how much of his success is due to what she was to him. Two days before his death he said to me, "I have to thank God for the happiest of homes, and the sweetest of wives."

Many will remember with gratitude the little home in Charlotte Street, as the scene of some of the pleasantest and most refreshing hours they have ever known. John Sedding had the gift of attracting young men, artists and others, to himself, and of entering speedily into the friendliest relations with them. He met them with such taking frankness, such unaffected warmth of welcome, that they surrendered to him at once, and were at once at ease with him and happy.

On Sundays, when the religious duties of the day were over, he was wont to gather a certain number of these young fellows to spend the evening at his house. No one of those who were privileged to be of the party can forget the charming hospitality of these evenings. The apparatus was so simple, the result so delightful; an entire absence of display, and yet no element of perfect entertainment wanting. On these occasions, when supper was over, Mrs. Sedding usually played for us with great discernment and feeling the difficult music of Beethoven, Grieg, Chopin, and others, and sometimes she sang. More than one friendship among their guests grew out of these happy evenings.

In course of time the increase of his family and the concurrent increase of his practice obliged him to remove, first his office to Oxford Street, and later on his home to the larger, purer air of a country house in the little village of West Wickham, Kent. This house he continued to occupy until his death. Work of all kinds now began to flow in upon him, not rapidly, but by steady increase. His rich faculty of invention, his wide knowledge, his skill in the manipulation of natural forms, the fine quality of his taste, were becoming more and more known. He produced in large numbers designs for wall-papers, for decoration, and for embroidery. These designs were never repetitions of old examples, nor were they a réchauffé of his own previous work. Something of his soul he put into all that he undertook, hence his work was never commonplace, and scarcely needed signature to be known as his, so unmistakably did it bear his stamp, the "marque de fabrique," of his individuality.

I have known few men so well able as he to press flowers into all manner of decorative service, in metal, wood, stone or panel, and in needlework. He understood them, and could handle them with perfect ease and freedom, each flower in his design seeming to fall naturally into its appointed place. Without transgressing the natural limits of the material employed, he yet never failed to give to each its own essential characteristics, its gesture, and its style. Flowers were indeed passionately loved, and most reverently, patiently studied by him. He would spend many hours out of his summer holiday in making careful studies of a single plant, or spray of foliage, painting them, as Mr. Ruskin had taught him, in siena and white, or in violet-carmine and white. Leaves and flowers were, in fact, almost his only school of decorative design.

This is not the place to attempt any formal exposition of John Sedding's views on Art and the aims of Art. They can be found distinctly stated and amply, often brilliantly, illustrated in his Lectures and Addresses, of which some have appeared in the architectural papers and some are still in manuscript.* But short of this formal statement, it may prove not uninteresting to note some characters of his work which impressed us.

Following no systematic order, we note first his profound sympathy with ancient work, and with ancient work of all periods that might be called periods of living Art. He never lost an opportunity of visiting and intently studying ancient buildings, sketching them, and measuring them with extraordinary care, minuteness, and patience. "On one occasion," writes Mr. Lethaby, "when we were hurried he said, 'We cannot go, it is life to us.'" A long array of sketch-books, crowded with studies and memoranda, remains to bear witness to his industry. In spite of this extensive knowledge, and copious record of old work, he never literally reproduced it. The unacknowledged plagiarisms of Art were in his judgment as dishonest as plagiarisms in literature, and as hopelessly dead. "He used old forms," writes Mr. Longden, "in a plastic way, and moulded them to his requirements, never exactly reproducing the old work, which he loved to draw and study, but making it his starting-point for new developments. This caused great difference of opinion as to the merit of his work, very able and skilful judges who look at style from the traditional point of view being displeased by his designs, while others who may be said to partake more of the movement of the time, admired his work."

His latest and most important work, the Church of the Holy Trinity, Sloane Street, is a case in point. It has drawn out the most completely opposed judgments from by no means incompetent men; denounced by some, it has won the warmest praise from others, as, for instance, from two men who stand in the very front rank of those who

---

* It is much to be wished that these Lectures and Addresses should be collected and published.

excel, William Morris has said of it, "It is on the whole the best modern interior of a town church"; and the eminent painter, E. Burnes-Jones, writing to John Sedding, writes: "I cannot tell you how I admire it, and how I longed to be at it." Speaking further of this sympathy with old work, Mr. Longden, who knew him intimately, and worked much with him, writes, "The rather rude character of the Cornish granite work in the churches did not repel him, indeed, he said he loved it, because he understood it. He has made additions to churches in Cornwall, such as it may well be imagined the old Cornishmen would have done, yet with an indescribable touch of modernness about them. He also felt at home with the peculiar character of the Devonshire work, and some of his last work is in village churches where he has made a rather ordinary church quite beautiful and interesting, by repairing and extending old wooden screens, putting in wooden seats, with an endless variety of symbolic designs, marble font and floor, fine metal work, simple but well-designed stained glass, good painting in a reredos, all, as must be with an artist, adding to the general effect, and falling into place in that general effect, while each part is found beautiful and interesting, if examined in detail."

"The rich Somersetshire work, where the fine stone lends itself to elaborate carving, was very sympathetic to Sedding, and he has added to and repaired many churches in that county, always taking the fine points in the old work and bringing them out by his own additions, whether in the interior or the exterior, seizing upon any peculiarity of site or position to show the building to the best advantage, and never forgetting the use of a church, but increasing the convenience of the arrangements for worship, and emphasizing the sacred character of the buildings on which he worked."

In his lectures to Art students, no plea was more often on his lips than the plea for living Art, as contrasted with "shop" Art, or mere antiquarianism. The artist is the product of his own time and of his own country, his nature comes to him out of the past, and is nourished in part upon the past, but he lives in the present, and of the present, sharing its spirit and its culture. John Sedding had great faith in the existence of this art gift, as living and active in his own time, he recognised it reverently and humbly in himself, and looked for it and hailed it with joy and generous appreciation in others. Hence the value he set upon association among Art workers. "Les gens d'esprit," says M. Taine, speaking of Art in Italy, "n'ont jamais plus d'esprit que lorsqu'ils sont ensemble. Pour avoir des œuvres d'art il faut d'abord des artistes, mais aussi des ateliers. Alors il y avait des ateliers, et en outre les artistes faisaient des corporations. Tous se tenaient, et dans la grande société, de petites sociétés unissaient étroitement et librement leurs membres. La familiarité les rapprochait ; la rivalité les aiguillonnait."*

He gave practical effect to these views in the conduct of his own office, which was as totally unlike the regulation architect's office, as life is unlike clockwork.

Here is a charming "interior" from the pen of his able chief assistant and present successor, Mr. H. Wilson :—

"I shall not readily forget my first impressions of Mr. Sedding. I was introduced to him at one of those delightful meetings of the Art Workers' Guild, and his kindly reception of me, his outstretched hand, and the unconscious backward impulses of his head, displaying the peculiar whiteness of the skin over the prominent temporal and frontal bones, the playful gleam of his eyes as he welcomed me, are things that will remain with me as long as memory lasts.

"Soon after that meeting I entered his office, only to

---

* *Philosophie de l'art en Italie* (p. 162).— H. TAINE.

find that he was just as delightful at work as in the world.

"The peculiar half shy yet eager way in which he rushed into the front room, with a smile and a nod of recognition for each of us, always struck me. But until he got to work he always seemed preoccupied, as if while apparently engaged in earnest discussion of some matter an undercurrent of thought was running the while, and as if he were devising something wherewith to beautify his work even when arranging business affairs.

"This certainly must have been the case, for frequently he broke off in the midst of his talk to turn to a board and sketch out some design, or to alter a detail he had sketched the day before with a few vigorous pencil-strokes. This done, he would return to business, only to glance off again to some other drawing, and to complete what would not *come* the day before. In fact he was exactly like a bird hopping from twig to twig, and from flower to flower, as he hovered over the many drawings which were his daily work, settling here a form and there a moulding as the impulse of the moment seized him.

"And though at times we were puzzled to account for, or to anticipate his ways, and though the work was often hindered by them, we would not have had it otherwise.

"Those 'gentillesses d'oiseaux,' as Hugo says, those little birdy ways, so charming from their unexpectedness, kept us constantly on the alert, for we never quite knew what he would do next. It was not his custom to move in beaten tracks, and his everyday life was as much out of the common as his inner life. His ways with each of us were marked by an almost womanly tenderness. He seemed to regard us as his children, and to have a parent's intuition of our troubles, and of the special needs of each with reference to artistic development.

"He would come, and taking possession of our stools

would draw with his left arm round us, chatting cheerily, and yet erasing, designing vigorously meanwhile. Then, with his head on one side like a jackdaw earnestly regarding something which did not quite please him, he would look at the drawing a moment, and pounce on the paper, rub all his work out, and begin again. His criticism of his own work was singularly frank and outspoken even to us. I remember once when there had been a slight disagreement between us, I wrote to him to explain. Next morning, when he entered the office, he came straight to the desk where I was working, quietly put his arm round me, took my free hand with his and pressed it and myself to him without a word. It was more than enough.

He was, however, not one of those who treat all alike. He adapted himself with singular facility to each one with whom he came in contact; his insight in this respect was very remarkable, and in consequence he was loved and admired by the most diverse natures. The expression of his face was at all times pleasant but strangely varied, like a lake it revealed every passing breath of emotion in the most wonderful way, easily ruffled and easily calmed.

"His eyes were very bright and expressive, with long lashes, the upper lids large, full, and almost translucent, and his whole face at anything which pleased him lit up and became truly radiant. At such times his animation in voice, gesture, and look was quite remarkable, his talk was full of felicitous phrases, happy hits, and piquant sayings.

"His was the most childlike nature I have yet seen, taking pleasure in the simplest things, ever ready for fun, trustful, impulsive, and joyous, yet easily cast down. His memory for details and things he had seen and sketched was marvellous, and he could turn to any one of his many sketches and find a tiny scribble made twenty or thirty years ago, as easily as if he had made it yesterday.

"His favourite attitude in the office was with his back to the fireplace and with his hands behind him, head thrown back, looking at, or rather through one. He seldom seemed to look at anyone or anything, his glance always had something of divination in it, and in his sketches, however slight, the soul of the thing was always seized, and the accidental or unnecessary details left to others less gifted to concern themselves with.

"His love of symbolism was only equalled by his genius for it, old ideas had new meanings for him, old symbols were invested with deeper significance and new ones full of grace and beauty discovered. In this his intense, enthusiastic love of nature and natural things stood him in good stead, and he used Nature as the old men did, to teach new truths. For him as well as for all true artists, the universe was the living visible garment of God, the thin glittering rainbow-coloured veil which hides the actual from our eyes. He was the living embodiment of all that an architect should be, he had the sacred fire of enthusiasm within, and he had the power of communicating that fire to others, so that workmen, masons, carvers could do, and did lovingly for him, what they would not or could not do for others. We all felt and still feel that it was his example and precept that has given us what little true knowledge and right feeling for Art we may possess, and the pity is there will never be his like again.

"He was not one of those who needed to pray 'Lord, keep my memory green,' though that phrase was often on his lips, as well as another delightful old epitaph :

> 'Bonys emonge stonys lys ful steyl
> Quilst the soules wanderis where that God will.' "*

This delightful and assuredly entirely faithful picture

---

* In Thornhill Church.

is in itself evidence of the contagion of John Sedding's enthusiasm.

Beyond the inner circle of his own office, he sought and welcomed the unfettered co-operation of other artists in his work; in the words of a young sculptor, "he gave us a chance." He let them say their say instead of binding them to repeat his own. God had His message to deliver by them, and he made way that the world might hear it straight from their lips.

The same idea of sympathetic association, "fraternité généreuse — confiance mutuelle — communauté de sympathies et d'aspirations," has found embodiment in the Art Workers' Guild, a society in which artists and craftsmen of all the Arts meet and associate on common ground. John Sedding was one of the original members of this Guild, and its second Master.

Of his connection with the Guild the Secretary writes: "No member was ever more respected, none had more influence, no truer artist existed in the Guild." And Mr. Walter Crane: "His untiring devotion to the Guild throughout his term of office, and his tact and temper, were beyond praise."

It must not be inferred from these facts that John Sedding's sympathies were only for the world of Art, art-workers, and art-ideals. He shared to the full the ardour of his Socialist friends, in their aspirations for that new order of more just distribution of all that makes for the happiness of men, the coming "city which hath foundations whose builder and maker is God." He did not share their confidence in their methods, but he honoured their noble humanity, and followed their movements with interest and respect, giving what help he could. The condition of the poor, especially the London poor, touched him to the quick sometimes with indignation at their wrongs, sometimes with deep compassion and humbled admiration at the pathetic patience with which they bore the burden of their joyless, suffering lives. His own happy constitution and experience never led him to adopt the cheap optimism with which so many of us cheat our conscience, and justify to ourselves our own selfish inertness. The more ample income of his last years made no difference in the simple ordering of his household, it did make difference in his charities. He gave money, and what is better, gave his personal labour to many works for the good of others, some of which he himself had inaugurated.

John Sedding was an artist by a necessity of his nature. God made him so, and he could not but exercise his gift, but apart from the satisfaction that comes by doing what we are meant for, it filled him with thankfulness to have been born to a craft with ends so noble as are the ends of Art. To give pleasure and to educate are aims good indeed to be bound by, especially when by education we understand, not mind-stuffing, but mind-training, in this case the training of faculty to discern and be moved by the poetry, the spiritual suggestiveness of common everyday life. This brought his calling into touch with working folk.

As a man, John Sedding impressed us all by the singular and beautiful simplicity and childlikeness of his character, a childlikeness which never varied, and nothing, not even the popularity and homage which at last surrounded him, seemed able to spoil it. He never lost his boyish spontaneity and frankness, the unrestrained brightness of his manners and address, his boyish love of fun, and hearty, ringing laugh. Mr. Walter Crane speaks of his "indomitable gaiety and spirits which kept all going, especially in our country outings." "He always led the fun," writes Mr. Lethaby, "at one time at the head of a side at 'tug of war,' at another, the winner in an 'egg and spoon race.'" His very faults were the faults of childhood, the impulsiveness, the quick and unreflecting resentment against wrong, and the vehement denunciation of it. He trusted his instincts far more than his reason, and on the whole, his instincts served him right well, yet at times they failed him, as in truth they fail us all. There were occasions when a little reflection would have led him to see that his first rapid impressions were at fault, and so have spared himself and others some pain and misunderstanding. Let a thing appear to him false, unfair, or cowardly, he would lower his lance and dash full tilt at it at once, sometimes to our admiration, sometimes to our amusement when the appearance proved but a windmill in the mist, sometimes to our dismay when—a rare case—he mistook friend for foe.

No picture of John Sedding could be considered at all to represent him which failed to express the blameless purity of his character and conduct. I do not think the man lives who ever heard a tainted word from his lips. There was in him such depth and strength of moral wholesomeness that he sickened at, and revolted against the unseemly jest, and still more against the scenes, and experiences of the sensuous (to use no stronger word) upon which in the minds of some, the artist must perforce feed his gift. With his whole soul he repudiated the idea that Art grew only as a flower upon the grave of virtue, and that artists could, or desired to, lay claim to larger moral licence than other less imaginative men.

I have kept till last the best and deepest that was in him, the hidden root of all he was, the hallowing of all he did. I mean his piety—his deep, unfeigned piety. In his address at the annual meeting of the Confraternity of the Blessed Sacrament, a singularly outspoken and vigorous exhortation to laymen to keep their practice abreast of their faith, he used the following words: "In the wild scene of 19th century work, and thought, and passion, when old snares still have their old witchery, and new depths of wickedness yawn at our feet, when the world is so wondrous kind to tired souls, and neuralgic bodies, and itself pleads for concessions to acknowledged weakness; when unfaith is so like faith, and the devil freely suffers easy acquiescence in high gospel truth, and even holds a magnifying-glass that one may better see the sweetness of the life of the 'Son of Man,' it is well in these days of sloth, and sin, and doubt, to have one's energies braced by a 'girdle of God·' about one's loins! It is well, I say, for a man to have a circle of religious exercises that can so hedge him about, so get behind his life, and wind themselves by long familiarity into his character that they become part of his everyday existence—bone of his bone."

Out of his own real knowledge and practice he spoke these words. The "circle of religious exercise," the girdle of God, had become for him part of his everyday existence. I can think of no better words to express the unwavering consistency of his life. It is no part of my duty to tell in detail what and how much he did, and with what whole-heartedness he did it.

Turning to outward things, every associate of John Sedding knew his enthusiasm for the cause of the Catholic revival in the English Church. It supplied him with a religion for 'his whole nature. No trouble seemed too great on behalf of it, though often his zeal entailed upon him some material disadvantage. Again and again I have known him give up precious hours and even days in unremunerated work, to help some struggling church or mission, or some poor religious community. It was a joy to him to contribute anything to the beauty of the sanctuary or the solemnity of its offices. From the year 1878 to 1881 he was sidesman, from 1882 to 1889 churchwarden of St. Alban's, Holborn, doing his work thoroughly, and with conspicuous kindliness and courtesy. It was one of the thorns to the rose of his new life in the country that it obliged him to discontinue this office. For eleven years he played the organ on Sunday afternoons for a service for young men and maidens, few of whom can forget the extraordinary life and pathos that he was wont by some magic to put into his accompaniment to their singing.

This present year, 1891, opened full of promise for John Sedding. In a marvellously short time he had come hand over hand into public notice and public esteem, as a man from whom excellent things were to be expected,—things interesting, original, and beautiful. Mr. Burne Jones writes: "My information about Sedding's work is very slight,—my interest in him very great, and my admiration too, from the little I had seen. I know only the church in Sloane Street, but that was enough to fill me with the greatest hope about him . . . I saw him in all some half-dozen times—liked him instantly, and felt I knew him intimately, and was looking forward to perhaps years of collaboration with him."

Work brought work, as each thing he did revealed, to those who had eyes to see, the gift that was in him. At Art Congresses and all assemblies of Art Workers his co-operation was sought and his presence looked for, especially by the younger men, who hailed him and his words with enthusiasm. To these gatherings he brought something more and better than the sententious wisdom, the chill repression which many feel called upon to administer on the ground of their experience. Experience—"cette pauvre petite cabane construite avec les débris de ces palais d'or, et de marbre appelés nos illusions." He put something of the fire that was in him into the hearts that heard him, he made them proud of their cause and of their place in it, and hopeful for its triumph and their own success. It was a contribution of sunshine and fresh air, and all that is the complete opposite of routine, red-tape, and the conventional.

We who have watched his progress have noticed of late a considerable development in his literary power, a more marked individuality of style, a swifter and smoother movement, a richer vocabulary, and new skill in the presentation of his ideas. He was exceedingly happy in his illustrations of a principle, and his figures were always interesting, never hackneyed. A certain "bonhomie" in his way of putting things won willing hearers for his words, which seemed to come to meet us with a smile and open, outstretched hands, as the dear speaker himself was wont to do. Something of course of the living qualities of speech are lost when we can receive it only from the cold black and white of print, instead of winged and full of human music from the man's own lips. Yet, in spite of this, unless I am mistaken, readers of this book will not fail to find in it a good deal to justify my judgment.

It seems to have taken some of his friends by surprise that John Sedding should write on Gardens. They knew him the master of many crafts, but did not count Gardencraft among them. As a matter of fact, it was a love that appeared late in life, though all along it must have been within the man, for the instant he had a garden of his own the passion appeared full grown. Every evening between five and six, save when his work called him to distant parts, you might have seen him step quickly out of the train at the little station of West Wickham, run across the bridge, and greeting and greeted by everybody, swing along the shady road leading to his house. In his house, first he kissed his wife and children, and then supposing there was light and the weather fine, his coat was off and he fell to work at once with spade or trowel in his garden, absorbed in his plants and flowers, and the pleasant crowding thoughts that plants and flowers bring.

After supper he assembled his household to say evening prayers with them. When all had gone to rest he would settle himself in his little study and write, write,

write, until past midnight, sometimes past one, dashing now and again at a book upon his shelves to verify some one or other of those quaint and telling bits which are so happily inwoven into his text. One fruit of these labours is this book on Garden-craft.

But I have detained the reader long enough. All is by no means told, and many friends will miss, I doubt not, with disappointment this or that feature which they knew and loved in him. It cannot be helped. I have written as I could, not as I would, within the narrow limits which rightly bound a preface.

How the end came, how within fourteen days the hand of God took from our midst the much love, genius, beauty which His hand had given us in the person of John and Rose Sedding, a few words only must tell.

On Easter Monday, March 30th, John Sedding spent two hours in London, giving the last sitting for the bust which was being modelled at the desire of the Art Workers' Guild. The rest of the day he was busy in his garden. Next morning he left early for Winsford, in Somersetshire, to look after the restoration of this and some other churches in the neighbourhood. Winsford village is ten miles from the nearest railway station Dulverton; the road follows the beautiful valley of the Exe, which rising in the moors, descends noisily and rapidly southwards to the sea. The air is strangely chill in the hollow of this woody valley. Further, it was March, and March of this memorable year of 1891. Lines of snow still lay in the ditches, and in white patches on the northern side of hedgerows. Within a fortnight of this time men and cattle had perished in the snow-drifts on the higher ground.

Was this valley the valley of death for our friend, or were the seeds of death already within him? I know not. Next morning, Wednesday, he did not feel well enough to get up. His kind hostess, and host, the Vicar of the parish, did all that kindness—kindness made harder and therefore more kind by ten miles' distance from a railway station—could do. John sent for his wife, who came at once, with her baby in her arms. On Saturday at midnight he received his last Communion. The next day he seemed to brighten and gave us hopes. On Monday there was a change for the worse, and on Tuesday morning he passed away in perfect peace.

At the wish of his wife, his grave was prepared at West Wickham. The Solemn Requiem, by her wish also, was at the church he loved and served so well, St. Alban's, Holborn. That church has witnessed many striking scenes, but few more impressive than the great gathering at his funeral. The lovely children's pall that John Sedding had himself designed and Rose Sedding had embroidered, covered the coffin, and on the right of it in a dark mass were gathered his comrades of the Art Workers' Guild.

The tragedy does not end here. On that day week, at that very same hour and spot, beneath the same pall, lay the body of his dear and devoted wife.

Side by side, near the tall elms of the quiet Kentish churchyard, the bodies of John and Rose Sedding are sleeping. The spot was in a sense chosen by Rose Sedding, if we may use the term 'choice' for her simple wish that it might be where the sun shines and flowers will grow. The western slope of the little hill was fixed upon, and already the flowers they loved so well are blooming over them.

Among the papers of Rose Sedding was found, pencilled in her own handwriting, the following lines of a 17th century poet :

> " 'Tis fit one flesh one house should have,
> One tomb, one epitaph, one grave ;
> And they that lived and loved either
> Should dye, and lye, and sleep together."

How strange that the words should have found in her own case such exact fulfilment.

E. F. RUSSELL.

St. Alban's Clergy House,
    Brooke Street, Holborn.
       June, 1891.

CONTENTS.

CHAP.		PAGE
I.	The Theory of a Garden	1
II.	Art in a Garden	28
III.	Historical and Comparative Sketch	41
IV.	The Stiff Garden	70
V.	The "Landscape-Garden"	98
VI.	The Technics of Gardening	133
VII.	The Technics of Gardening (*continued*)	153

ON THE OTHER SIDE.

VIII.	A Plea for Savagery	183
IX.	In Praise of Both	202

LIST OF ILLUSTRATIONS.

Levens. View in Garden ...	Frontispiece
Levens. ,, ,, ,, ...	to face p. 22
No. 8.—A Garden Enclosed ...	,, 48
View of the Fountains of the Cordonata ...	,, 64
No. 1.—Plan of Rosary with Sundial ...	,, 156
Perspective View of Garden in Plan No. 1 ...	,, 156
No. 7.—Plan of Tennis Lawn, Terraces, and Flower Garden	,, 158
No. 5.—General Plan of the Great Hall of the Villa Borghese	,, 160
No. 3.—General Plan of the Pleasaunce, Villa Albani	,, 160
No. 4.—Plan showing Arrangement of Sunk Flower Garden ... ...·	,, 164
No. 2.—Plan of Sunk Flower Garden.—Perspective View	,, 166
Perspective View of Sunk Garden in Plan No. 2	,, 166
Perspective View of Part of Garden at Downes, Hayle	,, 170
Perspective View of Garden in Plan No. 6 ...	,, 180
No. 6.—Plan showing Arrangement for Fountain, Yew Walk, &c.	,, 180
Perspective View of a Design for a Garden, with Clipped Yew Hedges, &c.	,, 182

GARDEN-CRAFT.

CHAPTER I.

ON THE THEORY OF A GARDEN.

"Come hither, come hither, come hither;
 Here shall he see
 No enemy
 But winter and rough weather."

SOME subjects require to be delineated according to their own taste. Whatever the author's notions about it at starting, the subject somehow slips out of his grasp and dictates its own method of treatment and style. The subject of gardening answers to this description: you cannot treat it in a regulation manner. It is a discursive subject that of itself breeds laggard humours, inclines you to reverie, and suggests a discursive style.

This much in defence of my desultory essay. The subject, in a manner, drafts itself. Like the garden, it, too, has many aspects, many side-paths, that open out broken vistas to detach one's interest and lure from the straight, broad terrace-platform of orderly discourse. At first sight, perhaps, with the balanced beauty of the thing in front of you, carefully parcelled out and <u>enclosed, as all proper</u>

gardens are, the theme may appear so compact, that all meandering after side-issues may seem sheer wantonness. As you proceed, however, it becomes apparent that you may not treat of a garden and disregard the instincts it prompts, the connection it has with Nature, its place in Art, its office in the world as a sweetener of human life. True, the garden itself is hedged in and neatly defined, but behind the garden is the man who made it; behind the man is the house he has built, which the garden adorns; and every man has his humours; every house has its own conditions of plan and site; every garden has its own atmosphere, its own contents, its own story.

So now, having in this short preamble discovered something of the rich variety and many-sidedness of the subject, I proceed to write down three questions just to try what the yoke of classification may do to keep one's feet within bounds : (1) What is a garden, and why is it made? (2) What ornamental treatment is fit and right for a garden? (3) What should be the relation of the garden to the house?

Forgive me if, in dealing with the first point, I so soon succumb to the allurements of my theme, and drop into flowers of speech! To me, then, a garden is the outward and visible sign of man's innate love of loveliness. It reveals man on his artistic side. Beauty, it would seem, has a magnetic charm for him; and the ornamental display of flowers betokens his bent for, and instinctive homage of beauty. And to say this of man in one grade of life is to say it of all sorts and conditions of men; and to say it of one garden is to say it of all—whether the garden be the child of quality or of lowliness; whether it adorn castle, manor-house, villa, road-side cottage or signalman's box at the railway siding, or Japanese or British tea-garden, or Babylonian terrace or Platonic grove at Athens—in each case it was made for eye-delight at Beauty's bidding. Even the Puritan, for all his gloomy creed and bleak undecorated life, is Romanticist here; the hater of outward show turns rank courtier at a pageant of flowers: he will dare the devil at any moment, but not life without flowers. And so we have him lovingly bending over the plants of his home-garden, packing the seeds to carry with him into exile, as though these could make expatriation tolerable. "There is not a softer trait to be found in the character of these stern men than that they should have been sensible of their flower-roots clinging among the fibres of their rugged hearts, and have felt the necessity of bringing them over sea and making them hereditary in the new land." (Hawthorne, "Our Old Home," p. 77.)

But to take a higher point of view. A garden is, in many ways, the "mute gospel" it has been declared to be. It is the memorial of Paradise lost, the pledge of Paradise regained. It is so much of earth's surface redeemed from the scar of the fall:

"Who loves a garden still keeps his Eden."

Its territories stand, so to speak, betwixt heaven

and earth, so that it shares the cross-lights of each. It parades the joys of earth, yet no less hints the joys of heaven. <u>It tells of man's happy tillage of his plot of ground, yet blazes abroad the infinite abundance of God's wide husbandry of the world. It bespeaks the glory of earth's array, yet publishes its passingness.</u>*

Again. The punctual waking of the flowers to new life upon the ruin of the old is unfavourable to the fashionable theory of extinction, for it shows death as the prelude of life. Nevertheless, be it admitted, the garden-allegory points not all one way; it is, so to speak, a paradox that mocks while it comforts. For a garden is ever perplexing us with the "riddle of the painful earth," ever challenging our faith with its counter-proof, ever thrusting before our eyes the abortive effort, the inequality of lot (two roses on a single stem, the one full-blown, a floral paragon, the other dwarfed and withered), the permitted spite of destiny which favours the fittest and drives the weak to the wall—ever preaching, with damnable iteration, the folly of resisting the ills that warp life and blight fair promise.

And yet while this is so, the annual spectacle of spring's fresh repair—the awakening from winter's

---

* Think of "a paradise not like this of ours with so much pains and curiosity made with hands"—says Evelyn, in the middle of a rhapsody on flowers—"eternal in the heavens, where all the trees are trees of life, the flowers all amaranths; all the plants perennial, ever verdant, ever pregnant, and where those who desire knowledge may taste freely of the fruit of that tree which cost the first gardener and posterity so dear." (Sylva, "Of Forest-trees," p. 148.)

trance—the new life that grows in the womb of the tomb—is happy augury to the soul that passes away, immature and but half-expressed, of lusty days and consummate powers in the everlasting garden of God. It is this very garden's message, "the best is yet to be," that smothers the self-pitying whine in poor David Gray's Elegy* and braces his spirit with the tonic of a wholesome pride. To the human flower that is born to blush unseen, or born, perchance, not to bloom at all, but only to feel the quickening thrill of April-passion—the first sweet consciousness of life—the electric touch in the soul like the faint beatings in the calyx of the rose—and then to diè, to die "not knowing what it was to live"—to such seemingly cancelled souls the garden's message is "trust, acquiesce, be passive in the Master's hand: the game of life is lost, but not for aye—

> . . . "There is life with God
> In other Kingdom of a sweeter air:
> In Eden every flower is blown."

To come back to lower ground, a garden represents what one may call the first simplicity of

---

* "My Epitaph."
"Below lies one whose name was traced in sand—
He died, not knowing what it was to live;
Died while the first sweet consciousness of manhood
And maiden thought electrified his soul:
Faint beatings in the calyx of the rose.
Bewildered reader, pass without a sigh
In a proud sorrow! There is life with God,
In other Kingdom of a sweeter air;
In Eden every flower is blown. Amen."
DAVID GRAY ("A Poet's Sketch-book, R. Buchanan, p. 81.)

external Nature's ways and means, and the first simplicity of man's handling of them, carried to distinction. On one side we have Nature's "unpremeditated art" surpassed upon its own lines—Nature's tardy efforts and common elementary traits pushed to a masterpiece. On the other side is the callow craft of Adam's "'prentice han'," turned into scrupulous nice-fingered Art, with forcing-pits, glass-houses, patent manures, scientific propagation, and the accredited rules and hoarded maxims of a host of horticultural journals at its back.

Or, to run still more upon fancy. A garden is a place where these two whilom foes—Nature and man—patch up a peace for the nonce. Outside the garden precincts—in the furrowed field, in the forest, the quarry, the mine, out upon the broad seas—the feud still prevails that began as our first parents found themselves on the wrong side of the gate of Paradise. But

"Here contest grows but interchange of love"—

here the old foes have struck a truce and are leagued together in a kind of idyllic intimacy, as is witnessed in their exchange of grace for grace, and the crowning touch that each puts upon the other's efforts.

The garden, I have said, is a sort of "betweenity"—part heaven, part earth, in its suggestions; so, too, in its make-up is it part Nature, part man: for neither can strictly say "I made the garden" to disregard the other's share in it. True, that behind all the contents of the place sits primal

Nature, but Nature " to advantage dressed," Nature in a rich disguise, Nature delicately humoured, stamped with new qualities, furnished with a new momentum, led to new conclusions, by man's skill in selection and artistic concentration. True, that the contents of the place have their originals somewhere in the wild—in forest or coppice, or meadow, or hedgerow, swamp, jungle, Alp, or plain hill-side. We can run each thing to earth any day, only that a change has passed over them; what in its original state was complex or general, is here made a chosen particular; what was monotonous out there, is here mixed and contrasted; what was rank and ragged there, is here taught to be staid and fine; what had a fugitive beauty there, has here its beauty prolonged, and is combined with other items, made " of imagination all compact." Man has taken the several things and transformed them; and in th process they passed, as it were, through the crucible of his mind to reappear in daintier guise; in the process, the face of Nature became, so to speak, humanised: man's artistry conveyed an added charm.

Judged thus, <u>a garden is, at one and the same time, the response which Nature makes to man's overtures,</u> and man's answer to the standing challenge of open-air beauty everywhere. Here they work no longer in a spirit of rivalry, but for the attainment of a common end. We cannot dissociate them in the garden. A garden is man's transcript of the woodland world: it is <u>common vegetation ennobled</u>: outdoor scenery neatly writ in man's small hand.

It is a sort of twin-picture, <u>conceived of man in the studio of his brain, painted upon Nature's canvas with the aid of her materials</u>—a twin-essay where Nature's

> . . . . "primal mind
> That flows in streams, that breathes in wind"

supplies the matter, man the style. It is Nature's rustic language made fluent and intelligible—Nature's garrulous prose tersely recast—changed into imaginative shapes, touched to finer issues.

"What is a garden?" For answer come hither: be Fancy's guest a moment. Turn in from the dusty high-road and noise of practical things—for

> "Not wholly in the busy world, nor quite
> Beyond it, blooms the garden that I love";

descend the octagonal steps; cross the green court, bright with great urns of flowers, that fronts the house; pass under the arched doorway in the high enclosing wall, with its gates traceried with rival wreaths of beaten iron and clambering sprays of jasmine and rose, and, from the vantage-ground of the terrace-platform where we stand, behold an art-enchanted world, where the alleys with their giddy cunning, their gentle gloom, their cross-lights and dappled shadows of waving boughs, make paths of fantasy—where the water in the lake quivers to the wind's soft footprints, or sparkles where the swallows dip, or springs in jets out of shapely fountain, or, oozing from bronze dolphin's mouth, slides down among moss-flecked stones into a deep dark pool, and is seen anon threading with still foot the careless-careful curved banks fringed with flowering shrubs and trailing willows and brambles—where the flowers smile out of dainty beds in the sunny ecstasy of "sweet madness"— where the air is flooded with fragrance, and the mixed music of trembling leaves, falling water, singing birds, and the drowsy hum of innumerable insects' wings.

"What is a garden?" <u>It is man's report of earth at her best.</u> It is earth emancipated from the commonplace. Earth is man's intimate possession—Earth arrayed for beauty's bridal. It is man's love of loveliness carried to excess—man's craving for the ideal grown to a fine lunacy. It is piquant wonderment; culminated beauty, that for all its combination of telling and select items, can still contrive to look natural, debonair, native to its place. A garden is Nature aglow, illuminated with new significance. It is Nature on parade before men's eyes; Flodden Field in every parish, where on summer days she holds court in "lanes of splendour," beset with pomp and pageantry more glorious than all the kings'.

"Why is a garden made?" Primarily, it would seem, <u>to gratify man's craving for beauty.</u> <u>Behind fine gardening is fine desire.</u> It is a plain fact that men do not make beautiful things merely for the sake of something to do, but, rather, because their souls compel them. Any beautiful work of art is a feat, an assay, of human soul. Someone has said that "noble dreams are great realities"—this in praise of unrealised dreams; but here, in the fine garden, is the noble dream and the great reality.

Here it may be objected that the ordinary garden is, after all, only a compromise between the common and the ideal: half may be for the lust of the eye, yet half is for domestic drudgery; half is for beauty, half for use. The garden is contrived "a double debt to pay." Yonder mass of foliage that bounds the garden, with its winding intervals of turf and look of expansiveness, it serves to conceal villadom and the hulking paper-factory beyond; that rock-garden with its developed geological formation, dotted over with choice Alpine plants, that the stranger comes to see. It is nothing but the quarry from whence the stone was dug that built the house. Those banks of evergreens, full of choice specimens, what are they but on one side the screen to your kitchen stuff, and on the other side, the former tenant's contrivance to assist him in forgetting his neighbour? Even so, my friend, an it please you! You are of those who, in Sainte-Beuve's phrase, would sever a bee in two, if you could!

The garden, you say, is a compromise between the common and the ideal. Yet nobility comes in low disguises. We have seen that the garden is wild nature elevated and transformed by man's skill in selection and artistic concentration—wild things to which man's art has given dignity. The common flowers of the cottager's garden tell of centuries of collaboration. The flowers and shrubs and trees with which you have adorned your own grounds were won for you by the curiosity, the aspiration, the patient roaming and ceaseless research of a long list of old naturalists; the design of your garden, its picturesque divisions and beds, a result of the social sense, the faculty for refined enjoyment, the constructive genius of the picked minds of the civilised world in all ages. The methods of planting approved of to-day, carrying us back to the admirably-dressed grounds of the ancient castles and abbeys, to the love of woodland scenery, which is said to be a special characteristic of Teutonic people, which is evidenced in the early English ballads; to the slowly acquired traditions of garden-masters like Bacon, Temple, Evelyn, Gilpin, and Repton, as well as to the idealised landscapes of Constable, Gainsborough, Linnell, and Turner; it is, in fact, the issue of the practical insight, the wood-craft, and idealistic skill of untold generations.

In this matter of floral beauty and garden-craft man has ever declared himself a prey to the "malady of the ideal"; the Japanese will even combine upon his trees the tints of spring and autumn.* But everywhere, and in all ages of the civilised world, man spares no pains to acquire the choicest specimens, the rarest plants, and to give to each thing so acquired the ideally best expression of which it is capable. It is as though Eden-memories still

---

* "This strange combination of autumn and spring tints is a very usual sight in Japan. . . . It is worth noting that in Japan a tree is considered chiefly for its form and tint, not for use. . . . I heard the cherry-trees were now budding, so I hurried up to take advantage of them, and found them more beautiful than I had ever imagined. There are at least fifty varieties, from delicately tinted white and pink to the richest rose, almost crimson blossom."—Alfred East's "Trip to Japan," *Universal Review*, March, 1890.

haunted the race with the solicitude of an inward voice that refused to be silenced, and is satisfied with nothing short of the best.

And yet, as some may point out, this homage of beauty that you speak of is not done for nought; there enters into gardening the spirit of calculation. A garden is a kind of investment. The labour and forethought man expends upon it must bring adequate return. For every flower-bed he lays down, for every plant, or shrub, or tree put into the ground, his word is ever the same,

> "Be its beauty
> Its sole duty."

It was not simply to gratify his curiosity, to serve as a pretext for adventure, that the gardener of old days reconnoitred the globe, culled specimens, and spent laborious days in studying earth's picturesque points; it was with a view to the pleasure the things would ultimately bring. And why not! Had man not served so long an apprenticeship to Nature on her freehold estate, the garden would not so directly appeal to our imaginations and command our spirits. A garden reveals man as master of Nature's lore; he has caught her accents, rifled her motives; he has transferred her bright moods about his own dwelling, has tricked out an ordered mosaic of the gleanings of her woodland carpet; has, as it were, stereotyped the spontaneous in Nature, has entrapped and rendered beautifully objective the natural magic of the outer world to gratify the inner world of his own spirit.

The garden is, first and last, made "for delectation's sake."

So we arrive at these conclusions. A garden is made to express man's delight in beauty and to gratify his instincts for idealisation. But, lest the explanation savour too much of self-interest in the gardener, it may be well to say that the interest of man's investment of money and toil is not all for himself. What he captures of Nature's revenues he repays with usury, in coin that bears the mint-mark of inspired invention. This artistic handling of natural things has for result "the world's fresh ornament,"* and for plant, shrub, or tree subject to it, it is the crowning and completion of those hidden pos-

---

* "If you look into our gardens annexed to our houses" (says William Harrison in Holinshed's "Chronicles") "how wonderful is their beauty increased, not only with flowers, which Columella calleth *Terrena Sydera*, saying 'Pingit et in varias terrestria, sydera flores,' and variety of curious and costly workmanship, but also with rare and medicinable herbs. . . . How Art also helpeth Nature in the daily colouring, doubling and enlarging the proportions of our flowers it is incredible to report, for so curious and cunning are our gardeners now in these days that they presume to do, in a manner, what they list with Nature, and moderate her course in things as if they were her superiors. It is a world also to see how many strange herbs, plants, and annual fruits are daily brought unto us from the Indies, Americans, Taprobane, Canary Isles, and all parts of the world, the which, albeit that his respect of the constitutions of our bodies, they do not grow for us (because God hath bestowed sufficient commodities upon every country for her own necessity) yet for delectation's sake unto the eye, and their odoriferous savours unto the nose, they are to be cherished, and God also glorified in them, because they are His good gifts, and created to do man help and service. There is not almost one nobleman, gentleman, or merchant that hath not great store of these flowers, which now also begin to wax so well acquainted with our evils that we may almost account of them as parcel of our own commodities."—(From "Elizabethan England," p. 26-7.)

sibilities of perfection that have lain dormant in them since the world began.

An artist has been defined as one who reproduces the world in his own image and likeness. The definition is perhaps a little high-flown, and may confer an autobiographical value to an artist's performances that would astonish none more than himself. Yet if the thought can be truthfully applied anywhere, it is where it occurred to Andrew Marvell—in a garden.

> " The mind, that ocean where each kind
> Does straight its own resemblance find ;
> Yet it creates, transcending these,
> Far other worlds and other seas,
> Annihilating all that's made
> To a green thought in a green shade."

And where can we find a more promising sphere for artistic creation than a garden ? Do we boast of fine ideas and perceptions of beauty and powers of design ! Where can our faculties find a happier medium of expression or a pleasanter field for display than the garden affords ? Nay, to have the ideas, the faculties, and the chance of their exercise and still to hold back were a sin ! For <u>a garden is, so to speak, the compliment a man of ideas owes to Nature, to his friends, and to himself.</u>

Many are the inducements to gardening. Thus, if I make a garden, I need not print a line, nor conjure with the painter's tools, to prove myself an artist. Again, <u>a garden is the only form of artistic creation that is bound by the nature of things to be more lovely in realisation than in the designer's con-</u>

ception. It is no mere hint of beauty—no mere tickling of the fancy—that we get here, such as all other arts (except music) are apt to give you. Here, on the contrary, we are led straight into a world of actual delights patent to all men, which our eyes can see, and our hands handle. More than this; whilst in other spheres of labour the greater part of our life's toil and moil will, of a surety, end as the wise man predicted, in vanity and vexation of spirit, <u>here is instant physical refreshment in the work the garden entails</u>, and, in the end, <u>our labour will be crowned with flowers.</u>

Nor have I yet exhausted the scene of a garden's pleasures. A man gets undoubted satisfaction in the very expression of his ideas—"the joy of the deed"—in the sense of Nature's happy response, the delight of creation,* the romance of possibility.

Some joy shall also come of the identity of the gardener with his creation.† He is at home here. He is intimate with the various growths. He carries in his head an infinity of details touching the welfare of the garden's contents. He participates in the life

* Here is Emerson writing to Carlyle of his "new plaything"—a piece of woodland of forty acres on the border of Walden Pond. "In these May mornings, when maples, poplars, walnut, and pine are in their spring glory, I go thither every afternoon and cut with my hatchet an Indian path thro' the thicket, all along the bold shore, and open the finest pictures." (John Morley's Essays, "Emerson," p. 304.) But, as Mr. Morley points out, he finds the work too fascinating, eating up days and weeks; "nay, a brave scholar should shun it like gambling, and take refuge in cities and hotels from these pernicious enchantments."

† "I like your Essays," said Henry the Third to Montaigne. "Then, sire, you will like me. I am my Essays."

of his plants, and is familiar with all their humours; like a good host, he has his eye on all his company. He has fine schemes for the future of the place. The very success of the garden reflects upon its master, and advertises the perfect understanding that exists between the artist and his materials. The sense of ownership and responsibility brings him satisfaction, of a cheaper sort. His the hand that holds the wand to the garden's magic; his the initiating thought, the stamp of taste, the style that gives it circumstance. Let but his hand be withdrawn a space, and, at this signal, the gipsy horde of weeds and briars—that even now peer over the fence, and cast clandestine seeds abroad with every favouring gust of wind—would at once take leave to pitch their tents within the garden's zone, would strip the place of art-conventions, and hurry it back to its primal state of unkempt wildness.

Someone has observed that when wonder is excited, and the sense of beauty gratified, there is instant recreation, and a stimulus that lifts one out of life's ordinary routine. This marks the function of a garden in a world where, but for its presence, the commonplace might preponderate; 'tis man's recreation-ground, children's fairyland, bird's orchestra, butterfly's banquet. Verse and romance have done well, then, to link it with pretty thoughts and soft musings, with summer reveries and moonlight ecstasies, with love's occasion, and youth's yearning. No fitter place could well be found than this for the softer transactions of life that awaken love, poesy, and passion. Indeed, were its winsomeness not balanced by simple human enjoyments—were its charmed silences not broken by the healthy interests of common daily life—the romps of children, the clink of tea-cups, the clatter of croquet-mallets, the *mêlée* of the tennis-courts, the fiddler's scrape, and the tune of moving feet, it might well seem too lustreful a place for this work-a-day world.

Apart from its other uses, there is no spot like a garden for cultivating the kindly social virtues. Its perfectness puts people upon their best behaviour. Its nice refinement secures the mood for politeness. Its heightened beauty produces the disposition that delights in what is beautiful in form and colour. Its queenly graciousness of mien inspires the reluctant loyalty of even the stoniest mind. Here, if anywhere, will the human hedgehog unroll himself and deign to be companionable. Here friend Smith, caught by its nameless charm, will drop his brassy gabble and dare to be idealistic; and Jones, forgetful of the main chance and "bulls" and "bears," will throw the rein to his sweeter self, and reveal that latent elevation of soul and tendency to romance known only to his wife!

"There be delights," says an ancient writer, "that will fetch the day about from sun to sun, and rock the tedious year as in a delightful dream." This tells, in terse English, the pleasures of a garden and the instincts that are gratified in its making. For a garden is Arcady brought home. It is man's bit of gaudy make-believe—his well-disguised fiction of an unvexed Paradise—standing witness of his quest of the ideal—his artifice to escape the materialism of a world that is too actual and too much with him. A well-kept garden makes credible to modern eyes the antique fable of an unspoiled world—a world where gaiety knows no eclipse, and winter and rough weather are held at bay. In this secluded spot the seasons slip by unawares. The year's passing-bell is ignored. Decay is cheated of its prize. The invading loss of cold, or wind, or rain—the litter of battered Nature—the "petals from blown roses on the grass"—the pathos of dead boughs and mouldering leaves, the blighted bloom and broken promise of the spring, autumn's rust or winter's wreckage are, if gardeners be brisk sons of Adam, instantly huddled out of sight, so that, come when you may, the place wears a mask of steady brightness; each month has its new dress, its fresh counterfeit of permanence, its new display of flowers or foliage, as pleasing, if not so lustrous as the last, that serves in turn to prolong the illusion and to conceal the secret irony and fond assumption of the thing.

> "I think for to touche also
> The world which neweth everie daie,
> So far as I can, so as I maie."

This snatch of Gower's rhyme expresses in old phrase the gardener's desire, or clothed in modern prose by Mr. Robinson ("English Flower-Garden," Murray), it is "to make each place at various seasons, and in every available situation, an epitome of the great flower-garden of the world."

We hinted a moment ago of the interest that a garden gathers from the mark of man's regard and tendence; and if this be true of a modern garden, how much more true of an old one! Indeed, this is undeniable in the latter case, for Time is ever friendly to gardens. Ordinarily his attitude towards all that concerns the memories of man is that of a jealous churl. Look at history. What is history but one long record of men who, in this sphere or that, have toiled, striven, sold their souls even, to perpetuate a name and have their deeds written upon the tablets of eternity, not reckoning upon the "all-oblivious enmity" of Time, who, with heedless hand, cuts their past into fragments, blots out their name, confuses their story, and frets with gnawing tooth each vestige of their handiwork. How, then, we ask—

> "How with this rage shall beauty hold a plea,
> Whose action is no stronger than a flower?"

Yet so it is. He who has no respect for antique glories, who snaps his fingers at earth's heroes, who overturns the statues of the laurelled Cæsars, encrusts the hieroglyphics of the Pharaohs, and commits their storied masonry to the mercies of the modern Philistine, will make exception in a garden. "Time's pencil" helps a garden. In a garden not only are the solemn shapes and passing conceits of grey epochs treasured up, even to their minutest particulars, but the drift of the years, elsewhere so disastrous, serves only to heighten their fascination and power of appeal.

Thus it comes to pass, that it were scarcely possible to name a more pathetic symbol of the past than an old garden,* nor a spot which, by its tell-tale shapes, sooner lends itself to our historic sense if we would recall the forms and reconstruct the life of our ancestors. For we have here the very setting of old life—the dressed stage of old drama, the scenery of old gallantry. Upon this terrace, in front of these flower-beds with these trees looking on, was fought out the old battle of right and wrong—here was enacted the heroic or the shameful deeds, the stirring or the humdrum passages in the lives of so many generations of masters, mistresses, children, and servants, who in far-off times have lived, loved, and died in the grey homestead hard by. "Now they are dead," as Victor Hugo says—"they are dead, but the flowers last always."

Admit, then, that for their secret quality, no less than for their obvious beauty, these old gardens should be treasured. For they are far more than they seem to the casual observer. Like any other piece of historic art, the old garden is only truly intelligible through a clear apprehension of the circumstances which attended its creation. Granted that we possess the ordinary smattering of historical

---

* Time does much for a garden. There is a story of an American plutocrat's visit to Oxford. On his tour of the Colleges nothing struck him so much as the velvety turf of some of the quadrangles. He asked for the gardener, and made minute enquiries as to the method of laying down, and maintaining the grass. "That's all, is it?" he exclaimed, when the process had been carefully described. "Yes, sir," replied the gardener with a twinkle in his eye, "That's all, but we generally leave it three or four centuries to settle down!"

knowledge, and the garden will serve to interpret the past and make it live again before our eyes. For the old place is (to use the journalist's phrase) an "object lesson" of old manners; it is a proof of ancient genius, a clue to old romance, a legacy of vague desire. The many items of the place—the beds and walks with their special trick of "style"— the parterre, the promenoir, the maze, the quincunx, the terraces, the extravagances in ever-green sculptures of which Pope spoke—what are they but the mould and figure of old-world thought, down to its most characteristic caprice! The assertive air of these things—their prominence in the garden-scenery—bespeak their importance in the scenery of old life. It was *thus* that our forefathers made the world about them picturesque, *thus* that they coloured their life-dreams and fitted an adjunct pleasure to every humour, *thus* that they climbed by flower-strewn stairs to the realm of the ideal and stimulated their sense of beauty.

And if further proof be needed of the large hold the garden and its contents had of the affections of past generations, we have but to turn to the old poets, and to note how the texture of the speech, the groundwork of the thought, of men like Milton, Herrick, Vaughan, Herbert, Donne (not to mention prose-writers) is saturated through and through with garden-imagery.

In the case of an old garden, mellowed by time, we have, I say, to note something that goes beyond mere surface-beauty. Here we may expect to find a certain superadded quality of pensive interest, which, so far as it can be reduced to words, tells of the blent influences of past and present, of things seen and unseen, of the joint effects of Nature and Man. The old ground embodies bygone conceptions of ideal beauty; it has absorbed human thought and memories; it registers the bequests of old time. Dead men's traits are exemplified here. The dead hand still holds sway, the pictures it conjured still endure, its cunning is not forgotten, its strokes still make the garden's magic, in shapes and hues that are unchanged save for the slow moulding of the centuries. *Really*, not less than metaphorically, the garden-growths do keep green the memories of the men and women who placed them there, as the flower that is dead still holds its perfume. And few will say that the chronicles of the dead do not

"Shine more bright in these contents
Than unwept stone besmeared with sluttish time."

There is a wealth of quiet interest in an old garden. We feel instinctively that the place has been warmed by the sunshine of humanity; watered from the secret spring of human joy and sorrow. Sleeping echoes float about its glades; its leafy nooks can tell of felicities sweeter than the bee-haunted cups of flowers; of glooms graver than the midnight blackness of the immemorial yews. It is their suggestion of antique experiences that endues the objective elements in an old garden like Haddon, or Berkeley, or Levens, or Rockingham, with a strange eloquence. The recollections of many a child have centred

Levens. View in Garden.

round these objects: the one touch of romance in a narrow, simple life is linked with them. Hearts danced or hearts drooped in this vicinity. Eyes that brimmed over with laughter or that were veiled with tears looked on these things as we look on them now—drank in the shifting lights and shadows on the grass—watched the waving of the cedar's dark layers of shade against an angry sky, "stern as the unlashed eye of God," and all the birds were silent—once took in the sylvan vistas of trees, lawn, fir-ridge, the broad-water where the coots and moor-hens now play (as then) among the green lily-pads and floating weeds, regardless of Regulas in lead standing in their midst; once dwelt upon the lustrous flower-beds, on the sun-dial on the terrace—noonday rendezvous of fantails—on the "Alley of Sighs," with its clipped beeches, its greystone seat half-way down, its rustle of dying leaves, and traditions of intrigue; on the lime avenue full of perfume in the sweet-o'-the-year, on the footbridge across the moat, on the streak of blue autumn mist that tracks the stream in yonder meadows where the landrail is croaking, and that brings magically near the beat of hoofs, the jingle of horses' bells, the rumble of homeward wagons on the road, and whifts of the reapers' songs; on the brief brilliance of the garden-panorama as the wintry-moon gives the black clouds the slip and suddenly discloses a white world of snow-muffled forms, that gleams with the eerie pallor of a ghost, and is as suddenly dissolved into darkness.

Simple sights, you will say, and familiar! and yet, when connected with some unique occasion, some epoch of a life, when seen on such a day, at such a supreme, all-absorbing moment from window, open door, terrace, arbour; in the stillness or in the wild rhetoric of the night, the familiar scene, momentarily flashed upon the brain's retina, may have subtly and unconsciously influenced the act, or coloured the thought of some human being, and the brand of that moment's impress may have accompanied that soul to the edge of doom.

Because of its hoarded memories we come to look upon an old garden as a sort of repository of old secrets; wrapped within its confines, as within the covers of a sacred book, repose so many pages of the sad and glad legend of humanity. We have before us the scenery of old home idylls, of old household reverences and customs, of old life's give and take—its light comedy or solemn farce, its dark tragedy, its summer masque, its stately dance or midnight frolic, its happy wedlock or its open sorrow, its endured wrong. The place is identified with the fortunes of old families: for so many generations has the old place been found favourable for lovers' tales, for youths' golden dreams, for girls' chime of fancy, for the cut and thrust of friendly wrangles, for the "leisures of the spirit" of student-recluse, for children's gambols and babies' lullabies. Seated upon this mossy bank, children have spelt out fairy tales, while birds, trees, brooks, and flowers listened together. The marvel of its cloistered grace has been

God-reminder to the saint; its green recesses have served for Enoch's walk,* for poet's retreat; as refuge for the hapless victim of broken endeavour; as enisled shelter for the tobacco-loving sailor-uncle with a wrecked fame; as invalid's Elysium; as haunt of the loafing, jesting, unambitioned man ("Alas, poor Yorick!"); as Death's sweet ante-room for slow-footed age.

What wonder that Sir William Temple devised that his heart should rest where its memories were so deep-intrenched—in his garden; or that Waterton should ask to be buried between the two great oaks at the end of the lake! (Norman Moore's Introduction to "Wanderings in South America.")

And if human affections be, as the poets declare, immortal, we have the reason why an old garden, in the only sense in which it ever is old, by the almanack, has that whisper and waving of secrecy, that air of watchful intentness, that far-reaching, mythological, unearthly look, that effect of being a kind of twilighted space common to the two worlds of past and present. Who will not agree with me in this? It matters not when you go there—at dawn, at noonday, no less than when the sky is murky and night-winds are sighing—and although you shall be the only visible human being present, it is not alone that you feel. A thrill comes over you, a mysterious sense warns you that this is none other

* "There is no garden well contrived, but that which hath an Enoch's walk in it."—SIR W. WALLER.

than the sanctuary of "the dead," as we call them; the place where, amid the hush of passionless existence, the wide leisure of uncounted time, the shades of once familiar presences keep their "tongueless vigil." They fly not at the "dully sound" of human footsteps; they ask no sympathy for regret which dare not tell the secret of its sorrow; but, with the gentle gait of old-world courtesy, they move aside, and when you depart resume occupation of ground which, for the sake of despairing wishes and memories of an uneffaced past, they may not quit. After life's fitful fever these waifs of a vanished world sleep not well; here are some consumed with covetousness, who are learning not to resent the word "mine" applied by the living owner of hall and garden, field and store; some that prey on withered bliss—the "bitter sweet of days that were"—this, the miser whose buried treasure lies undiscovered here, and who has nothing in God's bank in the other world; this, the author of the evil book; and this loveless, unlovely pair, the ruined and ruiner, yoked for aye; a motley band, forsooth, with "Satan's sergeants" keeping guard!

It is ever the indirect that is most eloquent. Someone says: Hence these tokens of a dead past open out vistas for one's imagination and drop hints of romance that would make thrilling reading in many volumes, but which shall never reach Mudie's.

Even Nature is not proof against the spell of an

old garden. The very trees have an "ancient melody of an inward agony":

> "The place is silent and aware
> It has had its scenes, its joys, and crimes,
> But that is its own affair"—

even Nature forgets to be her cold, impassive self, and puts on a sympathetic-waiting look in a spot so intricately strewn and meshed over with the fibres of human experience. Long and close intimacy with mankind under various aspects—witness of things that happened to squires, dames, priests, courtiers, servitors, page, or country-maid, in the roundabout of that "curious, restless, clamorous being which we call life"—has somehow tinged the place with a sensibility (one had almost said a *wizardry*) not properly its own. And this superadded quality reaches to the several parts of the garden and is not confined to the scene as a whole. Each inanimate item of the place, each spot, seems invested with a gift of attraction—to have a hidden tongue that could syllable forgotten names—to possess a power of fixing your attention, of fastening itself upon your mind, as though it had become, in a sense, humanised, and claimed kindred with you as related to that secret group with whose fortunes it was allied, with whose passions it had held correspondence, and were letting you know it could speak an if it would of

> "All the ways of men, so vain and melancholy."

CHAPTER II.

ON ART IN A GARDEN.

"O world, as God has made it! All is beauty."
                                        ROBERT BROWNING.

IN dealing with our second point—the ornamental treatment that is fit and right for a garden—we are naturally brought into contact with the good and bad points of both the old and the new systems of gardening. This being so, it may be well at once to notice the claims of the modern "Landscape-gardener" to monopolise to himself all the right principles of garden-craft: all other moods than his are low, all figures other than his are symbols of error, all dealings with Nature other than his are mere distortions.

If you have any acquaintance with books upon landscape-gardening written by its professors or their admirers, you will have learnt that in the first half of the eighteenth century, two heaven-directed geniuses — Kent and Brown — all of a sudden stumbled upon the green world of old England, and, perceiving its rural beauties, and the hitherto unexplored opportunities for ornamental display that the country afforded, these two put their heads together, and out of their combined cogitations sprang the English garden.

This, in brief, is what the landscape-gardener and his adherents say, and would have you believe; and, to prove their point, they lay stress upon the style of garden in vogue at the time Kent and Brown began their experiments, when, forsooth, traditional garden-craft was in its dotage and had lost its way in the paths of pedantry.

Should you, however, chance to have some actual knowledge of old gardens, and some insight into the principles which, consciously or unconsciously governed their making, it may occur to you to ask the precise points wherein the new methods claim to be different from the old, what sources of inspiration were discovered by the new school of gardeners that were not shared by English gardeners from time immemorial. Are there, then, *two* arts of gardening? or two sorts of Englishmen to please? Is not modern garden-craft identical with the old, so far, indeed, as it have art enough to stand any comparison with the other at all?

Let us here point to the fact, that <u>any garden whatsoever is but Nature idealised</u>, <u>pastoral scenery rendered in a fanciful manner.</u> It matters not what the date, size, or style of the garden, it represents an idealisation of Nature. *Real* nature exists outside the artist and apart from him. The Ideal is that which the artist conceives to be an interpretation of the outside objects, or that which he adds to the objects. The garden gives imaginative form to emotions the natural objects have awakened in man. The *raison d'être* of a garden is man's feeling the *ensemble*.

One fine day you take your architect for a jaunt along a country-lane, until stopping shyly in front of a five-barred gate, over which is nailed an ominous notice-board, you introduce him to your small property, the site of your new house. It is a field very much like the neighbouring fields—at least, so think the moles, and the rooks, and the rabbits; not you, for here is to be your "seat" for life; and before you have done with it, the whole country far and near will be taught to look as though it radiated round the site and the house you will build upon it—an honour of which, truth compels me to say, the land betrays not the remotest presentiment just now!

The field in question may be flat or undulating, it may be the lap of a hillside, the edge of a moor, a treeless stretch of furrowed land with traces of "rude mechanical's" usage, or suggestions of mutton or mangels. The particular character of the place, or its precise agricultural past, matters not, however; suffice it to say that it is a bit of raw, and more or less ungroomed, Nature.

Upon this plain, unadorned field, you set your man of imagination to work. He must absorb both it and its whole surroundings into his brain, and seize upon all its capabilities. He must produce symmetry and balance where now are ragged outlines of hillocks and ridges. He must trim and cherish the trees here, abolish the tree there; enlarge this slope, level that; open out a partial peep of blue distance here, or a gleam of silver water there. He must terrace the slope, step by step, towards the stream at the base, select the sunniest spots for the flower-beds, and arrange how best the gardens at their varying levels shall be approached or viewed from the house. In this way and that he must so manœuvre the perspective and the lights and shades, so compose or continue the sectional lines and general bearings of the ground as to enforce the good points that exist, and draw out the latent possibilities of the place, and this with as easy a hand, and as fine tact as the man can muster.

And now to come to our point. A dressed garden, I said, is Nature idealised—pastoral scenery put fancifully, in man's way. <u>A gardener is a master of what the French writer calls "the charming art of touching up the truth."</u>

Emerson observes that all the Arts have their origin in some enthusiasm; and the art of gardening has for its root, man's enthusiasm for the woodland world. It indicates a taste for flowers and trees and landscapes. It is admiration that has, so to speak, passed from the stage of emotion to that of form. A garden is the result of the emulation which the vision of beauty in the world at large is ever provoking in man—

"Straight mine eye hath caught new pleasures
While the landskip round it measures."

What of Nature has affected man on various

occasions, what has pleased his eye in different moods, played upon his emotions, pricked his fancy, suggested reverie, stirred vague yearnings, brought a sense of quickened joy—pastoral scenery, the music of leaves and waters, the hues and sweetness of country flowers, the gladness of colour, picturesque form of tree or contour of land, spring's bright laugh, autumn's glow, summer's bravery, winter's grey blanched face—each thing that has gone home to him has, in its way, fostered in man the garden mania. Inspired by their beauty and mystery, he has gathered them to himself about his home, has made a microcosm out of the various detached details which sum up the qualities, features, and aspects of the open country; and the art of this little recreated world is measured by the happy union of naturalness and of calculated effect.

What sources of inspiration were discovered by the new school of gardeners, I asked a moment ago, which were not spared by English gardeners from time immemorial? The art of gardening, I said, has its root in man's enthusiasm for the woodland world. See how closely the people of old days must have observed the sylvan sights of Nature, the embroidery of the meadows, the livery of the woods at different seasons, or they would not have been capable of building up that piece of hoarded loveliness, the old-fashioned English garden!

The pleasaunce of old days has been mostly stubbed up by the modern "landscape gardener," but if no traces of them were left we have still here and there the well-schemed surroundings of our English homes—park, avenue, wood, and water—the romantic scenery that hems in Tintern, Fountains, Dunster, to testify to the inborn genius of the English for planting. If the tree, shrub, and flower be gone from the grounds outside the old Tudor mansion, there still remains the blue-green world in the tapestries upon the walls, with their airy landscapes of trees and hills, hanging-gardens, flower-beds, terraces, and embowered nooks—a little fantastical it may be, but none the less eloquent of appreciation of natural beauty not confined to the gardener, but shared by the artist-maid, who

> . . . "with her neeld composes
> Nature's own shape, of bird, branch, or berry,
> That even Art sisters the natural roses."

And should these relics be gone, we still have the books in the library, rich in Nature-allusion. The simple ecstasies of the early ballad in the opening stanzas of "Robin Hood and the Monk"—

> "In somer when the shawes be sheyne,
> And leves be large and longe,
> Hit is full mery in feyre foreste
> To here the foulys song;
>
> To se the dere draw to the dale,
> And leve the hilles hee,
> And shadow hem in the leves grene,
> Under the grene-wode tre";

or in a "Musical Dreame"—

> "Now wend we home, stout Robin Hood,
> Leave we the woods behind us.
> Love passions must not be withstood,
> Love everywhere will find us.
> I livde in fielde and downe, and so did he;
> I got me to the woods, love followed me."

or shall we hear tell from Chaucer how

> "When that Aprille, with his showrës swoot
> The drought of March hath pierced to the root,
> . . . .
> Then longen folk to gone on pilgrimages."

Or hear from Stowe how the cockney of olden days "In the month of May, namely, on May-day in the morning, every man, except impediment, would walk in the sweet meddowes and green woods, ther to rejoyce their spirits with the beauty and savour of sweet flowers and with the harmonie of birds praysing God in their kinde."

Or shall we turn to Shakespeare's bright incidental touches of nature-description as in Perdita's musical enumeration of the flowers of the old stiff garden-borders "to make you garlands of," or the Queen's bit in "Hamlet," beginning

> "There is a willow grows aslant a brook,
> That shows his hoar leaves in the glassy stream."

Or to the old Herbals of Wyer, and Turner, and Gerard, whom Richard Jefferies* pictures walking about our English lanes in old days? "What wonderful scenes he must have viewed when they were all a tangle of wild flowers, and plants that are now scarce were common, and the old ploughs and the curious customs, and the wild red-deer—it would make a good picture, it really would, Gerard studying English orchids!"

Or shall we take down the classic volumes of Bacon, Temple, Evelyn, Cowley, Isaak Walton,

---
* "Field and Hedgerow," p. 27.

Gilbert White, each in his day testifying to the inborn love of the English for woodland scenery, their study of nature, and their taste in trees, shrubs, and flowers. What a vindication is here of the old-fashioned garden and gardener! What nonsense to set up Kent and Brown as the discoverers of the green world of old England, when, as Mr. Hamerton remarks in "The Sylvan Year" (p. 173), Chaucer hardly knows how or when to stop whenever he begins to talk about his enjoyment of Nature. "Chaucer," he says, "in his passion for flowers, and birds, and spring mornings in the woods, and by streams, is hard to quote, for he leads you down to the bottom of the page, and over the leaf, before you have time to pause."

The question now before us—" What ornament is fit and right for a garden?"—of itself implies a tendency to err in the direction of ornament. We see that on the face of it the transposition of the simple of Nature into the subtle of Art has its dangers. Something may be put, or something may be left, which were best absent. This may be taken as an established fact. In making a garden you start with the assumption that something must be sacrificed of wild Nature, and something must be superadded, and that which is superadded is not properly of this real, visible world, but of the world of man's brain.

The very enclosure of our garden-spaces signifies that Nature is held in duress here. Nature of herself cannot rise above Nature, and man, seeing perfections through her imperfections, capacities through her incapacities, shuts her in for cultivation, binds her feet, as it were, with the silken cord of art-constraint, and puts a gloss of intention upon her every feature.

In a garden Nature is not to be her simple self, but is to be subject to man's conditions, his choice, his rejection. Let us briefly see, now, what conditions man may fairly impose upon Nature—what lengths he may legitimately go in the way of mimicry of natural effects or of conventionalism. Both books and our own observation tell us that where the past generations of gardeners have erred it has been through a misconception of the due proportions of realism and of idealism to be admitted into a garden. At this time, in this phase, it was *Art*, in that phase it was *Nature*, that was carried too far; here design was given too much rein, there not rein enough, and people in their silly revolt against Art have gone straight for the "veracities of Nature," copying her features, dead or alive, outright, without discrimination as to their fitness for imitation, or their suitableness to the position assigned to them. To what extent, we ask, may the forms of Nature be copied or re-cast? What are the limits to which man may carry ideal portraiture of Nature for the purposes of Art? Questions like these would, of course, only occur to a curious, debating age like ours; but put this way or that they keep alive the eternal problems of man's standing to the world of Nature, the laws of idealism and realism, the nice distinctions of "more and less."

Now, it is not everything in Nature that can, or that may be, artificially expressed in a garden; nor are the things that it is permissible to use, of equal application everywhere. It were a palpable mistake, an artistic crime, so to speak, to follow the wild flights of Salvator Rosa and Gaspar Poussin, and with them to attempt a little amateur creation in the way of rent rocks, tumbled hillsides, and ruins that suggest a recent geological catastrophe, or antique monsters, or that imply by the scenery that we are living in the days of wattled abodes and savages with flint hatchets. Much, of course, may be done in this line in these days as in the past, if only one have sufficient audacity and a volcanic mind; yet, when it is done, both the value and the rightness of the art of the thing is questionable. "Canst thou catch Leviathan with a hook?" The primæval throes, the grand stupendous imagery of Nature should be held in more reverence. It were almost as fit to harness a polar bear to the gardener's mowing-machine as seek to appropriate the eerie phenomena of Nature in her untamed moods for the ornamental purposes of a garden. And as to the result of such work, the ass draped in the lion's skin, roaring horribly, with peaked snout and awkward shanks visible all the while, is not more ridiculous than the thinly-veiled savagery of an Italian garden of the seventeenth century.

Here, then, I think we have some guidance as to the principles which should regulate the choice of the " properties " that are fit for the scenic show of a garden. We should follow the dictates of good taste and of common sense. Of things applied direct from Nature the line should be drawn at the gigantesque, the elemental, the sad, the gruesome, the crude. True, that in art of another kind—in Architecture or in Music—the artistic equivalents of these qualities may find place, but as garden effects they are eminently unsuitable, except, indeed, where it is desired to perpetrate a grim joke.

Beyond these limitations, however, all is open ground for the imaginative handling of the true gardener; and what a noble residue remains! Nature in her health and wealth—green, opulent, lusty Nature is at his feet. Of things gay, debonair, subtle, and refined—things that stir poetic feelings or that give joy—he may take to himself and conjure with to the top of his bent. It is for him as for the poet in Sir Philip Sidney's words—" So as he goeth hand in hand with Nature, not enclosed within the narrow warrant of her gifts, but freely ranging within the zodiac of his own wit. Nature never set forth the earth in so rich tapestry as divers poets have done; neither with so pleasant rivers, fruitful trees, sweet-smelling flowers, nor whatsoever else may make the too-much loved earth more lovely: her world is brazen, *the poets only deliver a golden.*"

Animated with corresponding desire, the gardener resorts to lovely places in this "too-much loved earth," there to find his stock-in-trade and learn his craft. We watch him as he hies to the bravery of the spring-flowers in sunny forest-glades; to meadow-flats where lie the golden host of daffodils, the ladysmocks, and snake-spotted fritillaries ; we see him bend his way to the field of bluebells, the hill of primroses that with

> " their infinitie
> Make a terrestrial gallaxie
> As the smal starres do the skie ; "

we follow him to the tangled thicket with its meandering walks carpeted with anemones and hung over with sweet-scented climbers ; to the sombre boskage of the wood, where the shadows leap from their ambush in unexpected places and the brown bird's song floats upon the wings of silence: to the green dell with its sequestered pool edged round with alders, and willow-herb, and king-fern, and mountain-ash afire with golden fruit: to the cornfield "a-flutter with poppies": to the broad-terraced downs—its short, springy turf dotted over with white sheets of thorn-blossom: to the leaping, shining mountain-tarn that comes foaming out of the wood: to the pine-grove with its columned blackness and dense thatch of boughs that lisp the message of the wind, and " teach light to counterfeit a gloom "; to the widespread landscape with its undulating forest, its clumps of foliage, its gleams of white-beam, silver-birch, or golden yew, amid the dark blue of firs and hollies; its emerald meadows, yellow gorse-covers and purple heather ; the many tones of leafage in the spring and fall of the year.

And here I give but a few random sketches of Nature, taken almost at random from the portfolio of her painted delights—a dozen or more vignettes, shall we say?—ready-made for garden-distribution in bed, bank, wilderness, and park; things which the old gardener freely employed; features and images which he transferred to his dressed grounds, not copying them minutely but in an ideal manner; mixing his fancy with their fact, his compulsion with their consent; flavouring the simple with a dash of the strange and marvellous, combining dreams and actualities, things seen, with things born "within the zodiac of his own wit"; frankly throwing into the compacted glamour of the place all that will give *éclat* to Nature and teach men to apprehend new joy.

So, then, after separating the brazen from the golden in Nature—after excluding "properties" of the woodland world which are demonstrably unfit for the scenic show of a garden, how ample the scope for artistic creation in the things that remain! And, given an acre or two of land that has some natural capabilities, some charm of environment—given a generous client, a bevy of workmen, horses and carts, and, prime necessity of all, a pleasant homestead in the foreground to prompt its own adornment and be the centre of your efforts, and, upon the basis of these old tracks of Nature and old themes of Art, what may not one hope to achieve of pretty garden-effects that shall please the eye, flatter the taste, and captivate the imagination of such as love Beauty!

CHAPTER III.

HISTORICAL AND COMPARATIVE SKETCH OF THE ENGLISH GARDEN.

"The Earth is the garden of Nature, and each fruitful country a Paradise."—SIR THOMAS BROWNE.

IN the last chapter I observed that in dealing with our second point—the ornamental treatment that is fit for a garden—we should be brought into contact with the good and bad points of both the old and new systems of gardening. Hence the following discursus upon the historic English garden, which will, however, be as short as it can well be made, not only because the writer has no desire to wander on a far errand when his interest lies near home, but also because an essay, such as this, is ever bound to be an inconclusive affair; and 'twere a pity to lay a heavy burden upon a light horse!

At the outset of this section of our enquiry it is well to realise that there is little known about the garden of earlier date than the middle of the sixteenth century. Our knowledge of the mediæval garden is only to be acquired piecemeal, out of casual references in old chronicles, and stray pictures in illuminated manuscripts, and in each case allowance must be made for the fluent fancy of the artist. Moreover, early notices of gardens deal mostly with the orchard, or the vegetable or herb garden, where flowers grown for ornament occur in the borders of the ground.

It is natural to ascribe the first rudiments of horticultural science in this country to the Romans; and with the classic pastorals, or Pliny the Younger's Letter to Apollinaris before us, in which an elaborate garden is minutely and enthusiastically described, we need no further assurance of the fitness of the Roman to impart skilled knowledge in all branches of the science.

Loudon, in his noble "Arboretum et fruticetum Britannicum," enters at large into the question of what trees and shrubs are indigenous to Britain, and gives the probable dates of the introduction of such as are not native to this country. According to Whitaker, whose authority Loudon adopts, it would appear that the Romans brought us the plane, the box, the elm, the poplar, and the chestnut. (The lime, he adds, was not generally planted here till after the time of Le Nôtre: it was used extensively in avenues planted here in the reign of Charles the Second.) Of fruit trees, the Roman gave us the pear, the fig, the damson, cherry, peach, apricot, and quince. The aboriginal trees known to our first ancestors are the birch, alder, oak, wild or Scotch pine, mountain-ash or rowan-tree, the juniper, elder, sweet-gale, dog-rose, heath, St. John's wort, and the mistletoe.

Authorities agree in ascribing the introduction of many other plants, fruit trees, and trees of ornament or curiosity now common throughout England, to the monks. And the extent of our indebtedness to the monks in this matter may be gathered from the fact that monasteries abounded here in early times; and the religious orders have in all times been enthusiastic gardeners. Further be it remembered, many of the inmates of our monasteries were either foreigners or persons who had been educated in Italy or France, who would be well able to keep this country supplied with specimens and with reminiscences of the styles of foreign gardens up to date.

The most valuable authority on the subject of early English gardens is Alexander Necham, Abbot of Cirencester (1157-1217). His references are in the shape of notes from a commonplace-book entitled "Of the Nature of Things," and he writes thus: "Here the garden should be adorned with roses and lilies, the turnsole (heliotrope), violets and mandrake; there you should have parsley, cost, fennel, southernwood, coriander, sage, savery, hyssop, mint, rue, dittany, smallage, pellitory, lettuces, garden-cress, and peonies. . . . A noble garden will give thee also medlars, quinces, warden-trees, peaches, pears of St. Riole, pomegranates, lemons, oranges, almonds, dates, which are the fruits of palms, figs, &c."* Here, in truth, is a delightful medley of the useful and the beautiful, just like life! Yet the very use of the term "noble," as applied to a garden, implies that

* See "The Praise of Gardens."

even the thirteenth-century Englishman had a standard of excellence to stir ambition. Other garden flowers mentioned in Alexander's observations are the sunflower, the iris and narcissus.

The garden described by Necham bespeaks an amount of taste in the arrangement of the herbs, plants, and fruit-trees, but in the main it corresponds with our kitchen-garden. The next English writer upon gardens in point of date is Johannes de Garlandia, an English resident in France; but here is a description of the writer's garden at Paris. The ground here described consists of shrubbery, wood, grove, and garden, and from the account given it is inferred that both in matters of taste and in the horticultural and floral products of the garden, France had advanced farther than England in garden-craft in the fourteenth century, which is the date of the book.

In Mr. Hudson Turner's "Observations on the State of Horticulture in England"* in olden times he gives notices of the early dates in which the rose was under cultivation. In the thirteenth century King John sends a wreath of roses to his lady-love. Chronicles inform us that roses and lilies were among the plants bought for the Royal Garden at Westminster in 1276; and the annual rendering of a rose is one of the commonest species of quit-rent in ancient conveyances, like the "pepper-corn" of later times. The extent to which the culture of the rose was carried is inferred from the number of sorts

---

* "Archæological Journal," vol. v., p. 295.

mentioned in old books, which include the red, the sweet-musk, double and single, the damask, the velvet, the double-double Provence rose, and the double and single white rose. And the demand for roses seems to have been so great in old days that bushels of them frequently served as the payment of vassals to their lords, both in France and England. England has good reason to remember the distinction between the red and the white rose.

Of all the flowers known to our ancestors, the gilly-flower was perhaps the most common.

> "The fairest flowers o' the season
> Are our carnations and streak'd gilly flowers."
> *Winter's Tale.*

" Their use," says a quaint writer, "is much in ornament, and comforting the spirites by the sence of smelling." The variety of this flower, that was best known in early times, was the wall gilly-flower, or bee-flower. Another flower of common growth in mediæval gardens and orchards is the periwinkle.

> "There sprang the violet all newe,
> And fresh periwinkle, rich of hewe,
> And flowers yellow, white and rede,
> Such plenty grew there nor in the mede."

It is not considered probable that much art was expended in the laying out of gardens before the fifteenth century; but I give a list of illuminated MSS. in the Library of the British Museum, where may be found illustrations of gardens, and which I take from Messrs. Birch and Jenner's valuable Dic-

tionary of Principal Subjects in the British Museum*
under the head of Garden.

There is also a typical example of a fourteenth-century garden in the Romaunt d'Alexandre (Bodleian Library). Here the flower garden or lawn is separated by a wooden paling from the orchard, where a man is busy pruning. An old painting at Hampton Court, of the early part of the sixteenth century, gives pretty much the same class of treatment, but here the paling is decorated with a chevron of white and red colour.

To judge from old drawings, our forefathers seem to have been always partial to the greensward and trees, which is the landscape garden in the "egg"! A good extent of grass is always provided. Formal flower-beds do not often occur, and, where shown, they are sometimes surrounded by a low wattled fence—a protection against rabbits, probably. Seats and banks of chamomile are not unusual. A bank of earth seems to have been thrown up against the enclosing wall; the front of the bank is then faced with a low parti-

---

* "Early Drawings and Illuminations." Birch and Jenner. (Bagster, 1879, p. 134.)

"Gardens.

19 D. i. ff. I. etc.	15 E. iii. f. 122.
20 A. xvii. f. 7b.	15 E. vi. f. 146.
20 B. ii. f. 57.	16 G. v. f. 5.
14 803 f. 63.	17 F. i. f. 149 *b*.
18 851 f. 182.	19 A. vi. f. 2. 109.
18 852 f. 3. b.	19 C. vii. f. i.
26667 f. i.	20 C. v. ff. 7. *etc.*
Harl. 4425. f. 12. b.	Eg. 2022. f. 36. *h.*
Kings 7. f. 57.	Harl. 4425. f. 160 *b*.
6 E. ix. f. 15. b.	19720.
14 E. vi. f. 146.	19 A. vi. f. 109."

HISTORICAL AND COMPARATIVE.

tion of brick or stone, and the mould, brought to an even surface, is planted in various ways. Numerous illustrations of the fifteenth century give a bowling-green and butts for archery. About this date it is assumed the style of English gardening was affected by French and Flemish methods, which our connection with Burgundy at that time would bring about. To this period is also ascribed the introduction of the "mount" in England, although one would almost say that it is but a survival of the Celtic "barrow." It is a feature that came, however, into very common use, and is thus recommended by Bacon: "I wish also, in the very middle, a fair Mount, with three Ascents and Alleys, enough for four to walk abreast, which I would have to be perfect circles, without any Bulwarks or Imbossments, and the whole Mount to be thirty foot high, and some fine Banquetting House with some chimneys neatly cast, and without too much Glass."

The "mount" is said to have been originally contrived to allow persons in the orchard to look over the enclosing wall, and would serve not only as a place from which to enjoy a pretty view, but as a point of outlook in case of attack. Moreover, when situated in a park where the deer grazed, the unscrupulous sportsman might from thence shoot a buck. In early days the mounts were constructed of wood or of stone, and were curiously adorned within and without. Later on they resumed the old barrow shape, and were made of earth, and utilized for the culture of fruit trees. Lawson, an old writer of the sixteenth century, describes them as placed in divers corners of the orchard, their ascent being made by "stares of precious workmanship." When of wood, the mount was often elaborately painted.

An account of works done at Hampton Court in the time of Henry VIII., mentions certain expenses incurred for "anticke" works; and referring to Bailey's Dictionary, published early in the last century, the word "antick," as applied to curiously-shaped trees, still survives, and is explained as "odd figures or shapes of men, birds, beasts, &c., cut out." From the above references, and others of like nature, we know that the topiary art ("opus topiarum"), which dealt in quaintly-shaped trees and shrubs, was in full practice here throughout the latter half of the middle ages. Samuel Hartlib, in a book published in 1659, writes thus: "About fifty years ago Ingenuities first began to flourish in England." Lawson, writing in a jocose vein, tells how the lesser wood might be framed by the gardener "to the shape of men armed in the field ready to give battell; or swift-running greyhounds, or of well-sented and true-running hounds to chase the deere or hunt the hare"; adding as a recommendation that "this kinde of hunting shall not waste your corne, nor much your coyne!"

I find that John Leland in his Itinerary, 1540, further confirms the use of highly-decorated mounts: as at Wressel Castle, Yorkshire, he tells of the gardens with the mote, and the orchards as exceeding

No. 8. A Garden Enclosed.

fair; "and yn the orchardes were mounts writhen about with degrees, like the turnings in cokil shelles, to come to the top without payne." There is still to be seen, or according to Murray's Guide, 1876, was then to be seen, at Wotton, in Surrey, an artificial mount cut into terraces, which is a relic of Evelyn's work.

The general shape of an old-fashioned garden is a perfect square, which we take to be reminiscent of the square patch of ground which, in early days, was partitioned off for the use of the family, and walled to exclude cattle, or to define the property. It also repeats the quadrangular court of big Tudor houses. We may also assume that the shape would commend itself to the taste of the Renascence School of the Elizabethan and Jacobean eras, as being that of classic times; for the antique garden was fashioned in a square with enclosures of trellis-work, espaliers, and clipt box hedges, regularly ornamented with vases, fountains, and statuary.

The square shape was common to the French and Italian gardens also. Old views of Du Cerceau, an architect of the time of Charles IX. and Henry III., show a square in one part of the grounds and a circular labyrinth in another: scarcely a plot but has this arrangement. The point to note, however, is, that while the English garden might take the same general outline as the foreign, it had its own peculiarities; and although each country develops the fantastic ornament common to the stiff garden of the period in its own way, things are not carried to the same pitch of extravagant fancy in England as in France, Holland, or Italy.

Upon a general review of the subject of ornamental gardens, English and foreign, we arrive at the conclusion that the type of garden produced by any country is a question of soil and physical features, and a question of race. The character of the scenery of a country, the section of the land generally, no less than the taste of the people who dwell in it, prescribes the style of the type of garden. The hand of Nature directs the hand of Art.

Thus, in a hilly country like Italy, Nature herself prompts the division of the garden-spaces into wide terraces, while Art, on her side, provides that the terraces shall be well-proportioned as to width and height, and suitably defined by masonry walls having balustraded fronts, flights of steps, arcades, temples, vases, statues, &c.

Lady Mary Montagu's description of the *Giardino Jiusti* is a case in point: she depicts, as far as words can, how admirably it complies with the conditions of the scenery. The palace lies at the foot of a mountain "near three miles high, covered with a wood of orange, lemon, citron, and pomegranate trees, which is all cut up into walks, and divided into terraces that you may go into a separate garden from every floor of the house, diversified with fountains, cascades, and statues, and joined by easy marble staircases, which lead from one to another." It is a hundred years since this description was written, but the place is little altered to this day: "Who will now take the pains to climb its steep paths, will find the same charm in the aged cypresses, the oddly clipped ilexes and boxes, the stiff terraces and narrow, and now overgrown, beds."*

In France, where estates are larger, and the surface of the country more even and regular, the ornamental grounds, while following the Italian in certain particulars, are of wider range on the flat, and they attain picturesqueness upon lines of their own. The taste of the people, conveniently answering to the conditions of the country, runs upon long avenues and spacious grounds, divided by massive trellises into a series of ornamental sections—*Bocages, Cabinets de Verdure*, &c., which by their form and name, flatter the Arcadian sentiment of a race much given to idealisation. "I am making winding alleys all round my park, which will be of great beauty," writes Madame de Sévigné, in 1671. "As to my labyrinth, it is neat, it has green plots, and the palisades are breast-high; it is a lovable spot."

The French have parks, says the travelled Heutzner, but nothing is more different, both in compass and direction, than those common to England. In France they invented the parks as fit surroundings to the fine palaces built by Mansard and Le Nôtre, and the owners of these stately chateaux gratified their taste for Nature in an afternoon promenade on a broad stone terrace, gazing over a carved balustrade at a world made truly artificial to suit the period. The style of Le Nôtre is, in fact, based upon the

---

* "The Garden."—Walter Howe.

theory that Nature shall contribute a bare space upon which man shall lay out a garden of symmetrical character, and trees, shrubs, and flowers are regarded as so much raw material, out of which Art shall carve her effects.

Indeed, the desire for symmetry is carried to such extravagant lengths that the largest parks become only a series of square or oblong enclosures, regularly planted walks, bounded by chestnuts or limes; while the gardens are equally cut up into lines of trellises and palisades. In describing the Paris gardens Horace Walpole says, "they form light corridors and transpicuous arbours, through which the sunbeams play and checker the shade, set off the statues, vases, and flowers, that marry with their gaudy hotels, and suit the gallant and idle society who paint the walks between their parterres, and realise the fantastic scenes of Watteau and Durfé!" In another place he says that "many French groves seem green chests set upon poles. In the garden of Marshall de Biron, at Paris, consisting of fourteen acres, every walk is button-holed on each side by lines of flower-pots, which succeed in their seasons. When I saw it there were nine thousand pots of asters or la Reine Marguerite."

In Holland, which Butler sarcastically describes as

> "A land that rides at anchor, and is moor'd,
> In which they do not live, but go aboard"—

the conditions are not favourable to gardening. Man is here indebted to Nature, in the first place, for next to nothing: Air, Earth, and Water are, as it were, under his control. The trees grow, the rivers run, as they are directed; and the very air is made to pay toll by means of the windmills.

To begin with, Holland has a meagre list of indigenous trees and shrubs, and scarcely an indigenous ligneous flora. There is little wood in the country, for the heavy winds are calculated to destroy high-growing trees, and the roots cannot penetrate into the ground to any depth, without coming to water. The land is flat, and although artificial mountains of granite brought from Norway and Sweden have been erected as barriers against the sea, there is scarcely a stone to be found except in the Island of Urk.

The conditions of the country being so unfavourable to artistic handling, it needs a determined effort on man's part to lift things above the dead-level of the mean and commonplace. Yet see how Nature's defects may only prove Art's opportunity! Indeed, it is singular to note how, as it were, in a spirit of noble contrariness, the Dutch garden exhibits the opposite grace of each natural defect of the land. The great plains intersected with sullen watercourses yield up only slight strips of land, *therefore* these niggardly strips, snatched from "an amphibious world" (as Goldsmith terms it), shall be crammed with beauty. The landscape outside gapes with uniform dullness, *therefore* the garden within shall be spick and span. The flat treeless expanse outside offers no objects for measuring distance, *therefore* the perspective of the garden shall be a marvel of adroit planning and conjured proportions. The room is small, *therefore* its every inch shall seem an ell. The garden is a mere patch, *therefore* the patch shall be elaborately darned and pattern-stitched all over. The eye may not travel far, or can get no joy in a distant view, *therefore* it shall rest in pure content, focussed upon a scene where rich and orderly garniture can no farther go.

Thus have the ill-conditions of the land proved blessings in disguise. Necessity, the mother of invention, has produced the Dutch garden out of the most untoward geography, and if we find in its qualities and features traces of the conditions which surrounded its birth and development it is no wonder. Who shall blame the prim shapes and economical culture where even gross deception shall pass for a virtue if it be successful! Or the regular strips of ground, the long straight canals, the adroit vistas of grassy terraces long-drawn out, the trees ranged in pots, or planted in the ground at set intervals and carefully shorn to preserve the limit of their shade! Nay, one can be merciful to the garden's usual crowning touch, which you get at its far end—a painted landscape of hills and dales and clumps of trees to beguile the enamoured visitor into the fond belief that Holland is not Holland : and, in the foreground the usual smiling wooden boy, shooting arrows at nothing, happy in the deed, and tin hares squatting in likely nooks, whose shy hare eyes have worn the same startled gaze these sixty years or more, renewed with fresh paint from time to time as rust requires. Yet the Earth is richer and mankind happier for the Dutch garden!

And, as though out of compassion for the Dutchman's difficulties, kind Nature has put into his hands the bulb, as a means whereby he may attain the maximum of gaudy colour within the minimum of space. Given a few square yards of rescued earth and sufficient manure, and what cannot the neat-handed, frugal-minded, microscopic-eyed Dutchman do in the way of concentrated design with his bulbs, his clipt shrubs, his trim beds, his trickles of water, and strips of grass and gravel! And should all other resources fail he has still his pounded brick-dust, his yellow sand, his chips of ores and spars and green glass, which, though they may serve only remotely to suggest Nature, will at all events carry your mind off to the gay gardens of precious stones of fairy-land literature!

Indeed, once embarked upon his style of piquancy-at-any-price, and it is hard to see where the Dutch gardener need stop! In this sophisticated trifling—this lapidary's mosaic—this pastry-cook's decoration—this child's puzzle of coloured earth, substituted for coloured living flowers—he pushes Art farther than the plain Englishman approves. It is, however, only one step farther than ordinary with him. All his dealings with Nature are of this abstract sort: his details are clever, and he is ingenious, if not imaginative, in his wholes. Still, I repeat, the Earth is richer, and mankind happier for the Dutch garden. There is an obvious excuse for its over-fancifulness in George Meredith's remark that "dullness is always an irresistible temptation for brilliance." That the Dutchman should be thus able to compete with unfriendly Nature, and to reverse the brazen of the unkind land of his birth, is an achievement that reflects most creditably upon the artistic capacities of his nation.

But England—

"This other Eden, demi-paradise."—

suggests a garden of a less-constrained order than either of these. Not that the English garden is uniformly of the same type, at the same periods. The variety of the type is to be accounted for in two ways: firstly, by the ingrained eclecticism of the British mind; secondly, by the changeful character of the country—this district is flat and open, this is hilly—so that mere conformity to the lie of the land would produce gardens which belong now to the French type, now to the Italian. It is the same with British Art of all kinds, of all times: in days long before the Norman visitation and ever since, the English designer has leant more or less upon foreign initiative, which goes to prove either how inert is his own gift of origination, or how devious may be the tastes of a mixed race.

But if the English garden cannot boast of singular points of interest, if its art reflects foreign countries, it bears the mark of the English taste for landscape, which gives it distinction and is suggestive of very charming effects. The transcendent characteristic of the English garden is derived from and gets its impulse from the prevailing influence of Nature at home. It has the characteristics of the country.

It is, I know, commonly held now-a-days that the taste for landscape is wholly of modern growth. So far as England is concerned it came in, they say, with Thomson in poetry, and with Brown in gardens. So far as relates to the *conscious* relish for Nature, so far as relates to the love of Nature as a mirror of the moods of the mind, or as a refuge from man, this assertion may be true enough. Yet, surely the *conscious* delight in landscape must have been preceded by an *unconscious* sympathy this way : it could not have sprung without generation. Artistic sight is based upon instinct, feeling, perceptions that reach one knows not how far back in time, it does not come by magic.

See also what a rude, slatternly affair this much-lauded landscape-garden of the " immortal Brown " was! Here are two sorts of gardens—the traditional garden according to Bacon, the garden according to Brown. Both are Nature, but the first is Nature in an ideal dress, the second is Nature with no dress at all. The first is a garden for a civilised man, the second is a garden for a gipsy. The first is a picture painted from a cherished model, the second is a photograph of the same model undressed. Brown's work, in fact, represents the garden's return to its original barbaric self—the re-inauguration of the elemental. Let it not be said, then, that Brown discovered the model, for her fairness was an established fact or she would not have been so richly apparelled when he lighted upon her. In other words, the love of the Earth—"that green-tressed goddess," Coleridge calls her—was no new thing in Brown's day: the sympathy for the woodland world, the love of tree, flower, and grass is behind the manipulated stiff garden of the fifteenth and two succeeding centuries, and it is the abiding source of all enthusiasm in garden-craft.

How long this taste for landscape had existed in pre-Thomsonian days it does not fall to us to determine. Suffice it to say that so long as there has been an English school of gardening this sympathy for landscape has found expression in the English garden.* The high thick garden-walls of the old fighting-days shall have ample outlooks in the shape of "mounts," from whence views may be had of the open country. The ornamental value of forest trees is well-known and appreciated. Even in the thirteenth century the English gardener is on the alert for new specimens and "trees of curiosity," and he is a master of horticulture. In Chaucer's day he revels in the green-sward,

"Ful thikke of gras, ful softe and swete."

* "English scenery of that special type which we call homely, and of which we are proud as only to be found in England, is, indeed, the production of many centuries of that conservatism which has spared the picturesque timber, and of that affectionate regard for the future which has made men delight to spend their money in imprinting on the face of Nature their own taste in trees and shrubs." ("Vert and Venery," by Viscoun Lymington; *Nineteenth Century*, January, 1891.)

And the early ballads as I have already shown are full of allusion to scenery and woodland. In the days of fine gardens the Englishman must still have his four acres "to the green," his adjuncts of shrubbery, wilderness, and park. Nay, Henry VIII.'s garden at Nonsuch, had its wilderness of ten acres. "Chaucer opens his Clerke's Tale with a bit of landscape admirable for its large style," says Mr. Lowell, "and as well composed as any Claude" ("My Study Windows," p. 22). "What an airy precision of touch is here, and what a sure eye for the points of character in landscape." So, too, can Milton rejoice in

> "Nature boon
> Poured forth profuse on hill and dale and plain,"

and Herrick:

> "Sing of brooks, of blossoms, birds, and bowers,
> Of April, May, of June, and July flowers."

Nor is this taste for landscape surprising in a country where the natural scenery is so fair and full of meaning. There are the solemn woods, the noble trees of forest and park: the "fresh green lap" of the land, so vividly green that the American Hawthorne declares he found "a kind of lustre in it." There is the rich vegetation, and "in France, and still less in Italy," Walpole reminds us, "they could with difficulty attain that verdure which the humidity of our climate bestows." There are the leafy forest ways gemmed with flowers; the vast hunting-grounds of old kings, the woodland net of hazel coppice, the hills and dales, sunned or shaded, the plains mapped out with hedgerows and enlivened with the glitter of running water : the heather-clad moors, the golden gorse covers, the rolling downs dotted over with thorns and yews and chalk cliffs, the upland hamlets with their rosy orchards, the farm homesteads nestling in green combes, the grace of standing corn, the girdle of sea with its yellow shore or white, red, or grey rocks, its wolds and tracts of rough uncultivated ground, with bluffs and bushes and wind-harassed trees—Nature's own " antickes "—driven like green flames, and carved into grotesque shapes by the biting gales. There are the

> " Russet lawns, and fallows grey
> Where the nibbling flocks do stray,
> Mountains on whose barren breast
> The labouring clouds do often rest,
> Meadows prim with daisies pied,
> Shallow brooks and rivers wide "—

the land that Richard Jefferies says "wants no gardening, it *cannot* be gardened; the least interference kills it"—English woodland whose beauty is in its detail. There is nothing empty and unclothed here. Says Jefferies, " If the clods are left a little while undisturbed in the fields, weeds spring up and wild flowers bloom upon them. Is the hedge cut and trimmed, lo! the bluebells flower the more, and a yet fresher green buds forth upon the twigs." " Never was there a garden like the meadow," cries this laureate of the open fields; "there is not an inch of the meadow in early summer without a flower."

And if the various parts and details of an English

landscape are so beautiful in themselves, what shall we say of the scenery when Nature, turned artist, sweeps across it the translucent tints of dawn or sunset, or wind and cloud-fantasy; or veil of purple mist, or grey or red haze, or drift of rain-shower thrown athwart the hills, for the sunbeams to try their edge upon; or any of the numberless atmospheric changes, pure and tender, stern and imperious, that our humid climate has ever ready to hand!

Shut in, as we in England are, with our short breadths of view ("on a scale to embrace," remarks George Meredith), folded, as it were, in a field-sanctuary of Nature-life—girt about with scenery that is at once fair, compact, sweetly familiar and companionable, yet so changefully coloured, so full of surprises as the day jogs along to its evensong as to hold observation on the stretch, to force attention to Nature's last word, to fill the fallow-mind of lonely country folk with gentle wonder, and swell the "harvest of a quiet eye," is it strange that a land like ours should have bred an unrivalled school of Nature-readers among gardeners, painters, and poets? "As regards grandeur," says Hawthorne, "there are loftier scenes in many countries than the best that England can show; but, for the picturesqueness of the smallest object that lies under its gentle gloom and sunshine, there is no scenery like it anywhere." ("Our Old Home," p. 78.)

The *real* world of England, then, is, in the Englishman's opinion, itself so fair "it wants no gardening." Our school of gardeners seem to have found this out; for the task of the gardener has been rather that of translator than of creator; he has not had to labour at an artificial world he himself had made, but only to adorn, to interpret the world as it is, in all its blithe freedom. "The earth is the garden of Nature, and each fruitful country a Paradise;" and in England, "the world's best garden," man has only had to focus the view and frame it. Flowers, odours, dews, glistening waters, soft airs and sounds, noble trees, woodland solitudes, moonlight bowers, have been always with us.

It might seem ungenerous to institute a comparison between the French and English styles of gardening, and to put things in a light unfavourable to the foreigner, had not the task been already done for us by a Frenchman in a most out-spoken manner. Speaking of the French gardens, Diderot, in his Encyclopædia (*Jardin*) says: "We bring to bear upon the most beautiful situations a ridiculous and paltry taste. The long straight alleys appear to us insipid; the palisades cold and formless. We delight in devising twisted alleys, scroll-work parterres, and shrubs formed into tufts; the largest lots are divided into little lots. It is not so with a neighbouring nation, amongst whom gardens in good taste are as common as magnificent palaces are rare. In England, these kinds of walks, practicable in all weathers, seem made to be the sanctuary of a sweet and placid pleasure; the body is there relaxed, the mind diverted, the eyes are enchanted by the verdure of the turf and the bowling-greens; the variety of flowers offers pleasant flattery to the smell and sight, Nature alone, modestly arrayed, and never made up, there spreads out her ornaments and benefits. How the fountains beget the shrubs and beautify them! How the shadows of the woods put the streams to sleep in beds of herbage." This is poetry! but it is well that one French writer (and he so distinguished) should be found to depict an English garden, when architects like Jussieu and Antoine Richard signally failed to reproduce the thing, to order, upon French soil! And the *Petit Trianon* was in itself an improvement upon, or rather a protest against, the sumptuous splendour of the *Orangerie*, the basins of Latona and of Neptune, and the superb *tapis vert*, with its bordering groves of clipt trees and shrubs. Yet here is Arthur Young's unflattering description of the Queen's *Jardin Anglois* at Trianon: "It contains about 100 acres, disposed in the taste of what we read of in books of Chinese gardening, whence it is supposed the English style was taken. There is more of Sir William Chambers here than of Mr. Brown,[*] more effort than Nature, and more expence than taste. It is not easy to conceive anything that Art can introduce in a garden that is not here; woods, rocks, lawns, lakes, rivers, islands, cascades, grottoes,

---

[*] Miss Edwards (and I quote from her edition of Young's "Travels in France," p. 101) has a note to the effect that the Mr. Brown here referred to is "Robert Brown, of Markle, contributor to the *Edinburgh Magazine*, 1757-1831." Yet, surely this is none other than Mr. "Capability" Brown, discoverer of English scenery, reputed father of the English garden!

walks, temples, and even villages." Truly a *Jardin Anglois!*

We may well prefer Diderot's simile for the English garden as "the sanctuary of a sweet and placid pleasure" to the bustling crowd of miscellaneous elements that took its name in vain in the *Petit Trianon!*

For an English garden is at once stately and homely—homely before all things. Like all works of Art it is conventionally treated, and its design conscious and deliberate. But the convention is broad, dignified, quiet, homogeneous, suiting alike the characteristics of the country and of the people for whom it is made. Compared with this, the foreign garden must be allowed to be richer in provocation; there is distinctly more fancy in its conceits, and its style is more absolute and circumspect than the English. And yet, just as Browning says of imperfection, that it may sometimes mean "perfection hid," so, here our deficiencies may not mean defects.

In order that we may compare the English and foreign garden we must place them on common ground; and I will liken each to a pastoral romance. Nature is idealised, treated fancifully in each, yet how different the quality of the contents, the method of presentment, the style, the technique of this and that, even when the design is contemporaneous!

A garden is, I say, a sort of pastoral romance, woven upon a background of natural scenery. In the exercise of his pictorial genius, both the foreign and English artist shall run upon natural things, and

View of the Fountains of the Cordonata, and the ascent which goes up to the Broad Walk of Fountains, Villa Estense, Tivoli.

transcribe Nature imaginatively yet realisably; each composition shall have a pastoral air, and be rustic after its fashion. But how different the platform, how different the mental complexion, the technique of the artists! How different the detail and the atmosphere of the garden. The rusticity of the foreign garden is dished up in a more delectable form than is the case in the English, but there is not the same open-air feeling about this as about that; it does not convey the same sense of unexhausted possibilities—not the same tokens of living enjoyment of Nature, of heart-to-heart fellowship with her. The foreign garden is over-wrought, too full: it is a passionless thing—like the gaudy birds of India, finely plumed but songless; like the prize rose, without sweetness.

Of the garden of Italy, who shall dare to speak critically. Child of tradition: heir by unbroken descent, inheritor of the garden-craft of the whole civilised world. It stands on a pinnacle high above the others, peerless and alone: fit for the loveliest of lands—

. . "Woman-country, wooed not wed,
Loved all the more by Earth's male-lands,
Laid to their hearts instead"—

and it may yet be seen upon its splendid scale, splendidly adorned, with straight terraces, marble statues, clipped ilex and box, walks bordered with azalea and camellia, surrounded with groves of pines and cypresses—so frankly artistic, yet so subtly blending itself into the natural surroundings—into the distant plain, the fringe of purple hills, the gorgeous panorama of the Alps with its background of glowing sky. With such a radiant country to conjure with, we may truly say " The richly provided, richly require."

If we may speak our mind of the French and Dutch gardens, they in no wise satisfy English taste as regards their relation to Nature. Diderot has said that it is the peculiarity of the French to judge everything with the mind. It is from this standpoint that the Frenchman treats Nature in a garden. He is ever seeking to unite the accessory portions with the *ensemble*. He overdoes design. He gives you the impression that he is far more in love with his own ideas about Nature than with Nature herself; that he uses her resources not to interpret them or perfect them along their own lines, but express his own interesting ideas. He must provide stimulus for his imagination; his nature demands food for reverie, point for ecstasy, for delicious self-abandonment, for bedazzlement with ideal beauty, and the garden shall supply him with these whatever the cost to the materials employed. Hence a certain unscrupulousness towards Nature in the French garden; hence the daring picturesqueness, its legerdemain. Nature edited thus, is to the Englishman but Nature in effigy, Nature used as a peg for fantastical attire, Nature with a false lustre that tells of lead alloy—Nature that has forgotten what she is like.

In an English garden, as Diderot notes, Nature

is handled with more reverence, her rights are more respected. I am willing to allow that something of the reserve traceable in English art is begotten of the phlegmatic temper of the race that rarely gets beyond a quiescent fervour; and this temper, exhibited in a garden would incline us always to let well alone and not press things too hard. If the qualities of an English garden that I speak of are to be attributed to this temper, then, to judge by results, *laissez faire* is not a bad motto for the gardener! Certain it is that the dominance of man is more hinted at here than proclaimed. Compared with foreign examples we sooner read through its quaintnesses and braveries their sweet originals in Nature: nay, even when we have idealised things to our hearts' full bent, they shall yet retain the very note and rhythm of the woodland world from whence they sprang— "English in all, of genius blithely free." *

And this is true even in that extreme case, the Jacobean garden, where we have much the same quips and cranks, the same quaint power of metrical changes and playful fancy of the poetry of Herbert, Vaughan, Herrick, and Donne; even the little cleancut pedantries of this artfullest of all phases of English garden-craft make for a kind of bland stateliness and high-flown serenity, that bases its appeal upon placid beauty rather than upon mere ingenuity or specious extravagance. The conventionalities of its borders, its terraces and steps and images in lead or marble, its ornamental water, its trim geometrical

---

* Lowell's "Ode to Fielding."

patterns, its quincunx, clipped hedges, high hedges, and architectural adornments shall be balanced by great sweeps of lawn and noble trees that are not constrained to take hands, as in France, across the road and to look proper, but are left to grow large and thick and wide and free. True that there is about the Jacobean garden an air of scholarliness and courtliness; a flavour of dreamland, Arcadia, and Italy—a touch of the archaic and classical—yet the thing is saved from utter affectation by our English out-of-door life which has bred in us an innate love of the unconstrained, a sympathy that keeps its hold on reality, and these give an undefinable quality of freshness to the composition as a whole.*

To sum up. The main difference in the character of the English and the foreign schools of gardening lies in this, that the design of the foreign leans ever in the direction of artificiality, that of England towards natural freedom. And a true garden should have an equal regard for Nature and Art; it should represent a marriage of contraries, should combine finesse and audacity, subtilty and simplicity, the regular and the unexpected, the ideal and the real "bound fast in one with golden ease." In a French or Dutch garden the "yes" and "no"

---

* "Mr. *Evelyn* has a pleasant villa at *Deptford*," writes Gibson, "a fine garden for walks and hedges (especially his holly one, which he writes of in his "Sylva") . . In his garden he has four large round philareas, smooth-clipped, raised on a single stalk from the ground, a fashion now much used. *Part of his garden is very woody and shady for walking;* but his garden not being walled, has little of the best fruits."

of Art and Nature are always unequally yoked. Nature is treated with sparse courtesy by Art, its individuality is ignored, it sweats like a drudge under its load of false sentiment. "Sike fancies weren foolerie."

But in England, though we hold Nature in duress, we leave her unbound; if we mew her up for cultivation, we leave her inviolate, with a chance of vagrant liberty and a way of escape. Thus, you will note how the English garden stops, as it were, without ending. Around or near the house will be the ordered garden with terraces and architectural accessories, all trim and fit and nice. Then comes the smooth-shaven lawn, studded and belted round with fine trees, arranged as it seems with a divine carelessness; and beyond the lawn, the ferny heather-turf of the park, where the dappled deer browse and the rabbits run wild, and the sun-chequered glades go out to meet, and lose themselves "by green degrees" in the approaching woodland, —past the river glen, the steep fields of grass and corn, the cottages and stackyards and grey church tower of the village; past the ridge of fir-land and the dark sweep of heath-country into the dim waving lines of blue distance.

So that however self-contained, however self-centred the stiff old garden may seem to be, it never loses touch with the picturesque commonplaces of our land; never loses sympathy with the green world at large, but, in a sense, embraces and locks in its arms the whole country-side as far as eye can see.

CHAPTER IV.

HISTORICAL SKETCH—CONTINUED.

THE STIFF GARDEN.

"All is fine that is fit."

The English garden, as I have just tried to sketch it, was not born yesterday, the bombastic child of a landscape-gardener's recipe. It epitomises a nation's instincts in garden-craft; it is the slow result of old affection for, old wonder at, beauty in forms, colours, tones; old enthusiasm for green turf, wild flower, and forest tree. Take it at its best, it records the matured taste of a people of Nature-readers, Nature-lovers: it is that which experience has proved to be in most accord with the character and climate of the country, and the genius of the race.

Landscape has been from the first the central tradition of English art. Life spent amidst pictorial scenery like ours that is striking in itself and rendered more impressive and animated by the rapid atmospheric changes, the shifting lights and shadows, the life and movement in the sky, and the vivid intense colouring of our moist climate, has given our tastes a decided bent this way, and fashioned our Arts of Poetry, Painting, and Gardening. Out-of-door life among such scenery puts our senses on the alert, and the impressions of natural phenomena supplies our device with all its images.

The English people had not to wait till the eighteenth century to know to what they were inclined, or what would suit their country's adornment. From first to last, we have said, the English garden deals much with trees and shrubs and grass. The thought of them, and the artistic opportunities they offer, is present in the minds of accomplished garden-masters, travelled men, initiated spirits, like Sir Thomas More, Bacon, Shaftesbury, Temple, and Evelyn, whose aim is to give garden-craft all the method and distinctness of which it is capable. However saturated with aristocratic ideas the courtier-gardener may be, however learned in the circumspect style of the Italian, he retains his native relish for the woodland world and babbles of green fields. A sixteenth-century English gardener (Gerarde) adjured his countrymen to "Go forwarde in the name of God, graffe, set, plant, and nourishe up trees in every corner of your grounde." A seventeenth-century gardener (Evelyn) had ornamental landscape and shady woods in his garden as well as pretty beds of choice flowers.

"There are, besides the temper of our climate," writes another seventeenth-century garden-worthy (Temple), "two things particular to us, that contribute to the beauty and elegance of our gardens, which are the gravel of our walks and the fineness and almost perpetual greenness of our turf;

the first is not known anywhere else, which leaves all their dry walks in other countries very unpleasant and uneasy ; the other cannot be found in France or in Holland as we have it, the soil not admitting that fineness of blade in Holland, nor the sun that greenness in France during most of the summer." And following upon this is a long essay upon the ornamental disposition of the grounds in an English garden and the culture of fruit trees. " I will not enter upon any account of flowers," he says, "having only pleased myself with the care, which is more the ladies' part than the men's,* but the success is wholly in the gardener."

And Bacon is not so wholly enamoured of Arcadia and with the embodiment of far-brought fancies in his " prince-like " garden as to be callous of

---

* This remark of Temple's as to the small importance the flower-beds had in the mind of the gardener of his day, is significant : as indicating the different methods employed by the ancient and modern gardener. It was not that he was not "pleased with the care" of flowers, but that these were not his chiefest care ; his prime idea was to get broad, massive, well-defined effects in his garden generally. Hence the monumental style of the old-fashioned garden, the carefully-disposed ground, the formality, the well-considered poise and counterpoise, the varying levels and well-defined parts. And only inwoven, as it were, into the argument of the piece, are its pretty parts, used much as the jewellery of a fair woman. I should be sorry to be so unjust to the modern landscape gardener as to accuse him of caring over-much for flowers, but of his garden-device generally one may fairly say it has no monumental style, no ordered shape other than its carefully-schemed *disorder*. It is not a masculine affair, but effeminate and niggling ; a little park-scenery, curved shrubberies, wriggling paths, emphasised specimen plants, and flower-beds of more or less inane shape tumbled down on the skirts of the lawn or drive, that do more harm than good to the effect of the place, seen near or at a distance. How true it is that to believe in Art one must be an artist !

Nature's share therein. "The contents ought not well to be under thirty acres of ground, and to be divided into three parts; a green in the entrance, a heath or desert in the going forth, and the main garden in the midst, besides alleys on both sides; and I like well that four acres be assigned to the Green, six to the Heath, four and four to either side, and twelve to the main Garden. The Green hath two pleasures: the one, because nothing is more pleasant to the eye than green grass kept finely shorn; the other, because it will give you a fair alley in the midst, by which you may go in front upon a stately hedge, which is to enclose the garden." "For the heath, which was the third part of our plot, I wished it be framed as much as may be to a natural wildness," &c. Of which more anon.*

Whether the garden of Bacon's essay is the portrait of an actual thing, whether the writer—to use a phrase of Wordsworth—"had his eye upon the subject," or whether it was built in the man's brain like Tennyson's "Palace of Art," we cannot tell. From the singular air of experience that animates the description, the sure touch of the writer, we may infer that Gorhambury had some such garden, the fruit of its master's "Leisure with honour," or "Leisure without honour," as the case may be. But what seems certain is, that the essay is only a sign of the ordinary English gentleman's mind on the subject at that time; and in giving us this masterpiece, Bacon had no more notion of posing as the

* Nonsuch had its wilderness of ten acres.

founder of the English garden (*pace* Brown) than of getting himself labelled as the founder of Modern Science for his distinguished labours in that line. "I only sound the clarion," he says, "but I enter not into the battle."

Moderns are pleased to smile at what they deem the over-subtilty of Bacon's ideal garden. For my own part, I find nothing recommended there that a "princely garden" should not fitly contain (especially as these things are all of a-piece with the device of the period), even to those imagination-stirring features which one thinks he may have described, not from the life, but from the figures in "The Dream of Poliphilus" (a book of woodcuts published in Venice, 1499), features of the Enchanted Island, to wit the two fountains—the first to spout water, to be adorned with ornaments of images, gilt or of marble; the "other, which we may call a bathing-pool that admits of much curiosity and beauty wherewith we will not trouble ourselves; as that the bottom be finely paved with images, the sides likewise; and withal embellished with coloured glass, and such things of lustre; encompassed also with fine rails of low statues."

No artist is disposed to apologise for the presence of subtilty in Art, nor I for the subtle device of Bacon's garden. All Art is cunning. Yet we must not simply note the deep intent of the old master, but must equally recognise the air of gravity that pervades his recommendations—the sweet reason-

* *Nineteenth Century Magazine*, July, 1890.

ableness of suggestions for design that have as much regard for the veracities of Nature, and the dictates of common-sense, as for the nice elegancies and well-calculated audacities of consummate Art.

"I only sound the clarion, but I enter not into the battle." Even so, Master! we will hold thy hand as far as thou wilt go; and the clarion thou soundest right well, and most serviceably for all future gardeners!

I like the ring of stout challenge in the opening words, which command respect for the subject, and, if rightly construed, should make the heretic " landscape gardener,"—who dotes on meagre country-grass and gipsy scenery—pause in his denunciation of Art in a garden. "God Almighty first planted a Garden; and indeed it is the purest of humane pleasures. It is the greatest refreshment to the Spirits of man, without which Buildings and Palaces are but gross Handyworks. And a man shall ever see, that when ages grow to Civility and Elegancy, men come to build stately sooner than to garden finely: as if Gardening were the Greater Perfection."

This first paragraph has, for me, something of the stately tramp and pregnant meaning of the opening phrase of "At a Solemn Music." The praise of gardening can no further go. To say more were impossible. To say less, were to belittle your subject. I think of Ben Jonson's simile, "They jump farthest who fetch their race largest." For Bacon "fetches" his subject back to "In the beginning," and prophesies of all time. Thus does he lift his theme to its full height at starting, and the remainder holds to the same heroic measure.

If the ideal garden be fanciful, it is also grand and impressive. Nor could it well be otherwise. For when the essay was written fine gardening was in the air, and the master had special opportunities for studying and enjoying great gardens. More than this, Bacon was an apt craftsman in many fields, a born artist, gifted with an imagination at once rich and curious, whose performances of every sort declare the student's love of form, and the artist's nice discrimination of expression. Then, too, his mind was set upon the conquest of Nature, of which gardening is a province, for the service of man, for physical enjoyment, and for the increase of social comfort. Yet was he an Englishman first, and a fine gardener afterwards. Admit the author's sense of the delights of art-magic in a garden, none esteemed them more, yet own the discreet economy of his imaginative strokes, the homely bluntness of his criticisms upon foreign vagaries, the English sane-mindedness of his points, his feeling for broad effects and dislike of niggling, the mingled shrewdness and benignity of his way of putting things. It is just because Bacon thus treats of idealisms as though they were realisms, because he so skilfully wraps up his fanciful figures in matter-of-fact language that even the ordinary English reader appreciates the art of Bacon's stiff garden, and entertains art-aspirations unawares.

Every reader of Bacon will recognise what I wish to point out. Here, however, are a few examples:—

"For the ordering of the Ground within the Great Hedge, I leave it to a Variety of Device. Advising, nevertheless, that whatsoever form you cast it into; first it be not too busie, or full of work; wherein I, for my part, do not like Images cut out in Juniper, or other garden stuffs; *they are for Children.* Little low Hedges, round like Welts, with some pretty Pyramids, I like well; and in some places Fair Columns upon Frames of Carpenters' work. I would also have the Alleys spacious and fair."

"As for the making of Knots or Figures, with Divers Coloured earths, that they may lie under the windows of the House, on that side which the Garden stands, *they be but Toys, you may see as good sights many times in Tarts.*"

"For Fountains, they are a Great Beauty and Refreshment, *but Pools mar all, and make the Garden unwholesome and full of flies and frogs.*"

"For fine Devices, of arching water without spilling, and making it rise in several forms (of Feathers, Drinking Glasses, Canopies, and the like) (see "The Dream of Poliphilus") *they be pretty things to look on, but nothing to Health and Sweetness.*"

Thus throughout the Essay, with alternate rise and fall, do fancy and judgment deliver themselves of charge and retort, making a kind of logical see-saw. At the onset Fancy kicks the beam; at the middle, Judgement is in the ascendant, and before the sentence is done the balance rides easy. And this scrupulousness is not to be wholly ascribed to the fastidious bent of a mind that lived in a labyrinth; it speaks equally of the fineness of the man's ideal, which lifts his standard sky-high and keeps him watchful to a fault in attaining desired effects without running upon "trifles and jingles." The master-text of the whole Essay seems to be the writer's own apothegm: "Nature is commanded by obeying her."

That a true gardener should love Nature goes without saying. And Bacon loved Nature passionately, and gardens only too well. He tells us these were his favourite sins in the strange document —half prayer, half Apologia—written after he had made his will, at the time of his fall, when he presumably concluded that *anything* might happen. "Thy creatures have been my books, but Thy Scriptures much more. I have sought Thee in the courts, fields, and gardens, but I have found Thee in Thy temples."

Three more points about the essay I would like to comment upon. First, That in spite of its lofty dreaming, it treats of the hard and dry side of gardening as a science in so methodical a manner that but for what it contains besides, and for its mint-mark of a great spirit, the thing might pass as an extract from a more-than-ordinary practical gardener's manual. Bacon does not write upon the subject like a man in another planet, but like a man in a land of living men.

Secondly, As to the attitude of Bacon and his school towards external Nature. In them is no trace of the mawkish sentimentality of the modern "landscape-gardener," proud of his discoveries, bustling to show how condescending he can be towards Nature, how susceptible to a pastoral melancholy. There is nothing here of the maundering of Shenstone over his ideal landscape-garden that reads as though it would be a superior sort of pedants' Cremorne, where "the lover's walk may have assignation seats, with proper mottoes, urns to faithful lovers, trophies, garlands, etc., by means of Art"; and where due consideration is to be given to "certain complexions of soul that will prefer an orange tree or a myrtle to an oak or cedar." The older men thought first of the effects that they wished to attain, and proceeded to realise them without more ado. They had no "codes of taste" to appeal to, and no literary law-givers to stand in dread of. They applied Nature's raw materials as their art required. And yet, compared with the methods of the heavy-handed realist of later times such unscrupulousness had a merit of its own. To suit their purposes the old gardeners may have defied Nature's ways and wont; but, even so, they act as fine gentlemen should: they never pet and patronise her: they have no blunt and blundering methods such as mark the Nature-maulers of the Brown or Batty-Langley school: if they cut, they do not mince, nor hack, nor tear, they cut clean. In one's better moments one can almost sympathise with the "landscape-gardener's" feelings as he reads, if he ever does read, Evelyn's classic book "Sylva; or, a Discourse of Forest-trees," how they trimmed the hedges of hornbeam, "than which there is nothing more graceful," and the cradle or close-walk with that perplext canopy which lately covered the seat in his Majesty's garden at Hampton Court, and how the tonsile hedges, fifteen or twenty feet high, are to be cut and kept in order "with a scythe of four feet long, and very little falcated; this is fixed on a long sneed or straight handle, and *does wonderfully expedite the trimming of these and the like hedges.*"

Thirdly, Bacon's essay tells us all that an English garden *can* be, or *may* be. Bacon writes not for his age alone but for all time; nay, his essay covers so much ground that the legion of after-writers have only to pick up the crumbs that fall from this rich man's table, and to amplify the two hundred and sixty lines of condensed wisdom that it contains. Its category of effects reaches even the free-and-easy planting of the skirts of our dressed grounds, with flowers and shrubs set in the turf "framed as much as may be to a natural wildness"— a pretty trick of compromise which the modern book-writers would have us believe they invented themselves.

On one point the modern garden has the advantage and is bound to excel the old, namely in its employment of foreign trees and shrubs. The decorative use of "trees of curiosity," as the foreign trees were then called, and the employment of variegated foliage, was not unknown to the gardener of early days, but it was long before foreign plants were introduced to any great extent. Loudon has taken the trouble to reckon up the number of specimens that came to England century by century, and we gather from this that the imports of modern times exceed those of earlier times to an enormous extent. Thus, he computes that only 131 new specimens of foreign trees were introduced into England in the seventeenth century as against 445 in the following century.

Yet, to follow up this interesting point, we may observe that Heutzner, writing of English gardens in 1598, specially notes "the great variety of trees and plants at Theobalds."

Furthermore, to judge by Worlidge's "Systema Horticulturæ" (1677) it would seem that the practice of variegating, and of combining the variegated foliage of plants and shrubs, was in existence at that time.

"Dr. Uvedale, of Enfield, is a great lover of plants," says Gibson, writing in 1691, "and is become master of the greatest and choicest collection of exotic greens that is perhaps anywhere in this land. . . . His flowers are choice, his stock numerous, and his culture of them very methodical and curious; but to speak of the garden in the whole, it does not lie fine to please the eye, his delight and care lying more in the ordering particular plants, than in the pleasing view and form of his garden."

"*Darby*, at *Hoxton*, has but a little garden, but is master of several curious greens. . . . . His Fritalaria Crassa (a green) had a flower on it of the breadth of half-a-crown, like an embroidered star of many colours. . . . . He raises many striped hollies by inoculation," &c. ("Gleanings in Old Garden Literature," Hazlitt, p. 240.)

And yet one last observation I would like to make, remembering Bacon's subtilty, and how his every utterance is the sum of matured analytical thought. This yearning for wild nature that makes itself felt all through the Essay, this scheme for a "natural wildness" touching the hem of artificiality; this provision for mounts of some pretty height "to look abroad in the fields"; this care for the "Heath or Desart in the going forth, planted not in any order;" the "little Heaps in the Nature of Molehills (such as are in wild Heaths) to be set with pleasant herbs, wild thyme, pinks, periwinkle, and the like Low Flowers being withall sweet and sightly" —what does it imply? Primarily, it declares the artist who knows the value of contrast, the interest of blended contraries; it is the cultured man's hankering after a many-faced Nature readily accessible to him in his many moods; it tells, too, of the drift of the Englishman towards familiar landscape effects, the garden-mimicry which sets towards pastoral Nature; but above and beyond all else, it is a true Baconian stroke. Is not the man's innermost self here revealed, who in his eagerest moments struggled for detachment of mind, held his will in leash according to his own astute maxim "not to engage oneself too peremptorily in anything, but ever to have either a window open to fly out of, or a secret way to retire by"? In a sense, the garden's technique illustrates its author's personality. To change Montaigne's reply to the king who admired his essays, Bacon might say, "I am my garden."

Many references to old garden-craft might be given culled from the writings of Sir Thomas More, John Lyly, Gawen Douglas, John Gerarde, Sir Philip Sidney, and others; all of whom are quoted in Mr. Sieveking's charming volume, "The Praise of Gardens." But none will serve our purpose so well as the notes of Heutzner, the German traveller, who visited England in the 16th century, and Sir William Temple's description of the garden of Moor Park. According to Heutzner, the gardens at Theobalds, Nonsuch, Whitehall, Hampton Court, and Oxford were laid out with considerable taste and extensively ornamented with architectural and other devices. The Palace at Nonsuch is encompassed with parks full of deer, with delicious gardens, groves ornamented with trellis-work, cabinets of verdure, and walks enclosed with trees. "In the pleasure and artificial gardens are many columns and pyramids of marble, two fountains that spout water one round the other like a pyramid, upon which are perched small birds that stream water out of their bills. In the grove of Diana is a very agreeable fountain, with Actaeon turned into a stag, as he was sprinkled by the goddess and her nymphs, with inscriptions." Theobalds, according to Heutzner's account, has a "great variety of trees and plants," labyrinths, fountains of white marble, a summer-house, and statuary. The gardens had their terraces, trellis-walks, and bowling-greens, the beds being laid out in geometrical lines, and the hedges formed of yews, hollies, and limes, clipped and shaped into cones, pyramids, and other devices. Among the delights of Nonsuch was a wilderness of ten acres of extent. Of Hampton Court, he says: "We saw rosemary so planted and nailed to the walls as to cover them entirely, which is a method exceeding common in England."

No book on English gardens can afford to dispense with Temple's description of the garden of Moor Park, which is given with considerable relish, as though it satisfied the ideal of the writer.

"The perfectest figure of a Garden I ever saw, either at Home or Abroad."—" It lies on the side of a Hill (upon which the House stands), but not very steep. The length of the House, where the best Rooms and of most Use or Pleasure are, lies upon the Breadth of the Garden, the Great Parlour opens into the Middle of a Terras Gravel-Walk that lies even with it, and which may be, as I remember, about 300 Paces long, and broad in Proportion, the Border set with Standard Laurels, and at large Distances, which have the beauty of Orange-Trees, out of Flower and Fruit: From this Walk are Three Descents by many Stone Steps, in the Middle and at each End, into a very large Parterre. This is divided into Quarters by Gravel-Walks, and adorned with Two Fountains and Eight Statues in the several Quarters; at the End of the Terras-Walk are Two Summer-Houses, and the Sides of the Parterre are ranged with two large Cloisters, open to the Garden, upon Arches of Stone, and ending with two other Summer-Houses even with the Cloisters, which are paved with Stone, and designed for Walks of Shade, there are none other in the whole Parterre. Over these two Cloisters are two Terrasses covered with Lead and fenced with Balusters; and the Passage into these Airy Walks, is out of the two Summer-Houses, at the End of the first Terras-Walk. The Cloister facing the *South* is covered with Vines, and would have been proper for an Orange-House, and the other for Myrtles, or other more common Greens; and had, I doubt not, been cast for that Purpose, if this Piece of Gardening had been then in as much Vogue as it is now.

"From the middle of this Parterre is a Descent by many Steps flying on each Side of a Grotto, that lies between them (covered with Lead, and flat) into the lower Garden, which is all Fruit-Trees ranged about the several Quarters of a Wilderness, which is very Shady; the Walks here are all Green, the Grotto embellished with Figures of Shell-Rock work, Fountains, and Water-works. If the Hill had not ended with the lower Garden, and the Wall were not bounded by a Common Way that goes through the Park, they might have added a Third Quarter of all Greens; but this Want is supplied by a Garden on the other Side of the House, which is all of that Sort, very Wild, Shady, and adorned with rough Rock-work and Fountains." ("Upon the Garden of Epicurus, or of Gardening.")

The "Systema Horticulturæ" of John Worlidge (1677) was, says Mr. Hazlitt ("Gleanings in old Garden Literature," p. 40), apparently the earliest manual for the guidance of gardeners. It deals with technical matters, such as the treatment and virtue of different soils, the form of the ground, the structure of walls and fences, the erection of arbours, summer-houses, fountains, grottoes, obelisks, dials, &c.

"The Scots Gardener," by John Reid (1683) follows this, and is, says Mr. Hazlitt, the parent-production in this class of literature. It is divided into two portions, of which the first is occupied by technical instructions for the choice of a site for a garden, the arrangement of beds and walks, &c.

Crispin de Passe's "Book of Beasts, Birds, Flowers, Fruits, &c.," published in London (1630), heralds the changes which set in with the introduction of the Dutch school of design.

To speak generally of the subject, it is with the art of Gardening as with Architecture, Literature, and Music—there is the Mediæval, the Elizabethan, the Jacobean, the Georgian types. Each and all are

English, but English with a difference—with a declared tendency this way or that, which justifies classification, and illustrates the march of things in this changeful modern world.

The various types include the mediæval garden, the square garden, the knots and figures of Elizabethan times, with their occasional use of coloured earths and gravels; the pleach-work and intricate borders of James I.; the painted Dutch statues as at Ham House; the quaint canals, the winding gravel-walks, the formal geometrical figures; the quincunx and *étoile* of William and Mary; later on, the smooth, bare, and bald grounds of Kent, the photographic copyism of Nature by Brown, the garden-farm of Shenstone, and other phases of the "Landscape style" which served for the green grave of the old-fashioned English garden.

In the early years of George III. a reaction against tradition set in with so strong a current, that there remains scarcely any private garden in the United Kingdom which presents in all its parts a sample of the original design.

Levens, near Kendal, of which I give two illustrations, is probably the least spoiled of any remaining examples; and this was, it would seem, planned by a Frenchman, but worked out under the restraining influences of English taste. A picture on the staircase of the house, apparently Dutch, bears the inscription, "M. Beaumont, gardener to King James II. and Colonel James Grahme. He laid out the gardens at Hampton Court and at Levens." The gardener's house at the place is still called "Beaumont Hall." (See an admirable monograph upon "Col. James Grahme, of Levens," by Mr. Joscelin Bagot, Kendal.)

One who is perhaps hardly in sympathy with the quaintness of the gardens, thus writes: "There along a wide extent of terraced walks and walls, eagles of holly and peacocks of yew still find with each returning summer their wings clipt and their talons ; there a stately remnant of the old promenoirs such as the Frenchman taught our fathers,* rather I would say to *build* than plant—along which in days of old stalked the gentlemen with periwigs and swords, the ladies in hoops and furbelows—may still to this day be seen."

With the pictures of the gardens at Levens before us, with memories of Arley, of Brympton, of Wilton,† of Montacute, Rockingham, Penshurst, Severn End, Berkeley,‡ and Haddon, we may here pause a moment to count up and bewail our

---

* With regard to this remark, we have to note a certain amount of French influence throughout the reigns of the Jameses and Charleses. Here is Beaumont, "gardener to James II. ;" and we hear also of André Mollet, gardener to James I.; also that Charles II. borrowed Le Nôtre to lay out the gardens of Greenwich and St. James's Park.

† The gardens at Wilton are exceedingly beautiful, and contain noble trees, among which are a group of fine cedars and an ilex beneath which Sir Philip Sidney is supposed to have reclined when he wrote his "Arcadia" here. The Italian garden is one of the most beautiful in England.

‡ Of Berkeley, Evelyn writes : "For the rest the fore-court is noble, so are the stables ; and, above all, the gardens, which are incomparable by reason of the inequality of the ground, and a pretty *piscina*. The holly-hedges on the terrace I advised the planting of."

losses. Wolsey's garden at Hampton Court is now effaced, for the design of the existing grounds dates from William III. Nonsuch in Surrey, near Epsom race-course, is a mere memory. In old days this was a favourite resort of Queen Elizabeth; the garden was designed by her father, but the greater part carried out by the last of the Fitzalans. Evelyn, writing of Nonsuch, says: "There stand in the garden two handsome stone pyramids and the avenue planted with rows of fair elms, but the rest of these goodly trees, both of this and of Worcester Park adjoining, were felled by those destructive and avaricious rebels in the late war."

Theobalds, in Hertfordshire, had a noble garden; it was bought in 1564 by Cecil, and became the favourite haunt of the Stuarts, but the house was finally destroyed during the Commonwealth.

My Lord *Fauconbergh's* garden at *Sutton Court* is gone too. As described by Gibson in 1691, it had many charms. "The maze, or wilderness, there is very pretty, being set all with greens, with a cypress arbour in the middle," &c.

Sir *Henry Capell's* garden at Kew, described by the same writer, "has as curious greens, and is as well kept as any about London. . . His orange trees and other choice greens stand out in summer in two walks about fourteen feet wide, enclosed with a timber frame about seven feet high, and set with silver firs hedge-wise. . . His terrace walk, bare in the middle and grass on either side, with a hedge of rue on one side next a low wall, and a row of dwarf trees on the other, shews very fine; and so do from thence his yew hedges with trees of the same at equal distance, kept in pretty shapes with tonsure. His flowers and fruits are of the best, for the advantage of which two parallel walls, about fourteen feet high, were now raised and almost finished," &c.

Sir *Stephen Fox's* garden at *Chiswick*, "excels for a fair gravel walk betwixt two yew hedges, with rounds and spires of the same, all under smooth tonsure. At the far end of this garden are two myrtle hedges that cross the garden. The other gardens are full of flowers and salleting, and the walls well clad."

Wimbledon House, which was rebuilt by Sir Thomas Cecil in 1588, and surveyed by order of Parliament in 1649, was celebrated for its trees, gardens, and shrubs. In the several gardens, which consisted of mazes, wildernesses, knots, alleys, &c., are mentioned a great variety of fruit trees and shrubs, particularly a "faire bay tree," valued at £1; and "one very faire tree called the Irish arbutis, very lovely to look upon and worth £1 10s." (Lysons, I., 397.)

The gardens at Sherborne Castle were laid out by Sir Walter Raleigh. Coker, in his "Survey of Dorsetshire," written in the time of James I., says that Sir Walter built in the park adjoining the old Castle, "a most fine house which hee beautified with orchardes, gardens, and groves of much varietie and great delight; soe that whether that you consider the pleasantness of the seate, the goodnesse of the soyle, or the other delicacies belonging unto it, it rests unparalleled by anie in those partes" (p. 124). This same park, magnificently embellished with woods and gardens, was "improved" away by the "landscape-gardener" Brown, who altered the grounds.

Cobham, near Gravesend, still famous in horticultural annals as Nonsuch is for its apples, was the seat of the Brookes. The extent to which fruit was cultivated in old time is seen by the magnitude of the orangery at Beddington House, Surrey, which was two hundred feet long; the trees mostly measured thirteen feet high, and in 1690 some ten thousand oranges were gathered.

Ham is described with much gusto by Evelyn: "After dinner I walked to Ham to see the house and garden of the Duke of Lauderdale, which is indeed inferior to few of the best villas in Italy itself; the house furnished like a great Prince's, the parterres, flower-gardens, orangeries, groves, avenues, courts, statues, perspectives, fountains, aviaries, and all this at the banks of the sweetest river in the world, must needs be admirable."

Bowyer House, Surrey, is described also by Evelyn as having a very pretty grove of oaks and hedges of yew in the garden, and a handsome row of tall elms before the court. This garden has, however, made way for rows of mean houses.

At Oxford, where you would have expected more respect for antiquity, the walks and alleys, along which Laud had conducted Charles and Henrietta, the bowling-green at Christ Church of Cranmer's time—all are gone.

The ruthless clearance of these gardens of renown is sad to relate: "For what sin has the plough passed over your pleasant places?" may be demanded of numberless cases besides Blakesmoor. Southey, writing upon this very point, adds that "feeling is a better thing than taste,"—for "taste" did it at the bidding of critics who had no "feeling," and who veered round with the first sign of change in the public mind about gardening. Not content with watching the heroic gardens swept away, he must goad the Vandals on to their sorry work by flattering them for their good taste. For what Horace Walpole did to expose the poverty-stricken design and all the poor bankrupt whimsies of the garden of his day, we owe him thanks; but not for including in his condemnation the noble work of older days. In touching upon Lord Burleigh's garden, and that at Nonsuch, he says: "We find the *magnificent though false taste* was known here as early as the reigns of Henry VIII. and his daughter." This is not bad, coming from the man who built a cockney Gothic house adorned with piecrust battlements and lath-and-plaster pinnacles; who spent much of his life in concocting a maze of walks in five acres of ground, and was so far carried away by mock-rustic sentiment as to have rakes and hay-forks painted as leaning against the walls of his paddocks! But then Walpole, in his polished way, sneered at everybody and everything; he "spelt every man backward," as Macaulay observes; with himself he lived in eminent self-content.

So too, after quoting Temple's description of the garden at Moor Park with the master's little rhapsody—"the sweetest place I think that I have seen in my life, either before or since, at home or abroad"—Walpole has this icy sneer: "Any man might design and *build* as sweet a garden who had been born in and never stirred out of Holborn. It was not peculiar in Sir William Temple to think in that manner."

It is not wise, however, to lay too much stress upon criticisms of this sort. After all, any phase of Art does but express the mind of its day, and it cannot do duty for the mind of another time. "The old order changeth, yielding place to new," and to take a critical attitude towards the forms of an older day is almost a necessity of the case; they soon become curiosities. Yet we may fairly regret the want of tenderness in dealing with these gardens of the Elizabethan and Jacobean eras, for, by all the laws of human expression, they should be masterpieces. The ground-chord of the garden-enterprise of those days was struck by Bacon, who rates buildings and palaces, be they never so princely, as "but gross handiworks" where no garden is: "Men come to build stately sooner than to garden finely, as if gardening were the Greater Perfection"—the truth of which saying is only too glaringly apparent in the relative conditions of the arts of architecture and of gardening in the present day!

By all the laws of human expression, I say, these old gardens should be masterpieces. The sixteenth century, which saw the English garden formulated, was a time for grand enterprises; indeed, to this period is ascribed the making of England. These gardens, then, are the handiwork of the makers of England, and should bear the marks of heroes. They are relics of the men and women who made our land both fine and famous in the days of the Tudors; they represent the mellow fruit of the leisure, the poetic reverie, the patient craft of men versed in great affairs—big men, who thought and did big things—men of splendid genius and stately notions—past-masters of the art of life who would drink life to the lees.

As gardeners, these old statesmen were no dabblers. They had the good fortune to live in a current of ideas of formal device that touched art at all points and was well calculated to assist the creative faculty in design of all kinds. They lived before the art of bad gardening had been invented; before pretty thoughts had palled the taste, before gardening had learnt routine; while Nature smiled a virgin smile and had a sense of unsolved mystery. More than this, garden-craft was then no mere craze or passing freak of fashion, but a serious item in the round of home-life;—gardening was a thing to be done as well as it could be done. Design was fresh and open to individual treatment—men needed an outlet for their love of, their elation at, the sight of beautiful things, and behind them lay the background of far-reaching traditions to encourage, inspire, protect experiment with the friendly shadow of authority.

An accomplished French writer has remarked that even the modest work of Art may contain occasion for long processes of analysis. "Very great laws," he says, "may be illustrated in a very small compass." And so one thinks it is with the ancient garden. Looked at as a piece of design, it is the blossom of English genius at one of its sunniest moments. It is a bit of the history of our land. It embodies the characteristics of the mediæval, the Elizabethan and Jacobean ages just as faithfully as do other phases of contemporary art. It contains the same principle of beauty, the same sense of form, that animated these; it has the same curious turns of expression, the same mixture of pedantry and subtle sweetness; the same wistful daring and humorous sadness; the same embroidery of nice fancy—half jocund, half grave, as—shall we say— Shakespeare's plays and sonnets, Spenser's "Faërie Queene," Milton's "Comus," More's "Utopia," Bacon's Essays, Purcell's Madrigals, John Thorpe's architecture at Longleat. The same spirit, the same wit and fancy resides in each; they differ only in the medium of expression.

To condemn old English gardening, root and branch, for its "false taste" (and it was not peculiar to Walpole to think in that manner), was, in truth, to indict our nation on a line of device wherein we excelled, and to condemn device that represents the inspired dreams of some of England's elect sons.

To our sorry groundling minds the old pleasaunce may seem too rich and fantastic, too spectacular, too much idealised. And if to be English one must needs be *bourgeois*, the objection must stand. Here is developed garden-craft, and development almost invariably means multiplicity of forms and a marked departure from primæval simplicity. Grant, if you will, that Art is carried too far, and Nature not carried far enough in the old garden, yet did it deserve better treatment. Judged both from its human and its artistic side, the place is as lovable as it is pathetic. It has the pathos of all art that survives its creators, the pathos of all abandoned human idols, of all high human endeavour that is blown upon. What is more, it holds, as it were, the spent passion of men of Utopian dreams, the ideal (in one kind) of the spoiled children of culture, the knight-errantry of the Renascence—whose imagination soared after illimitable satisfaction, who were avowedly bent upon transforming the brazen of this world into the golden, to whom desire was but the first step to attainment, and failure an unknown experience.

But even yet some may demur that the interest of the antique garden, as we see it, is due to Nature direct, and not to art-agencies. It is Nature who gives it its artistic qualities of gradation, contrast, play of form and colour, the flicker of sunshine through the foliage, the shadows on the grass—not the master who begot the thing, for has he not been dead, and his vacant orbits choked with clay these two hundred years and more! To him, of course, may be ascribed the primal thought of the place, and, say, some fifty years of active participation in its ordering and culture, but for the rest—for its poetic excitement, for its yearly accesses of beauty—are they not to be credited in full to the lenience of Time and the generous operations of Nature?

Grant all that should rightly be granted to the disaffected grumbler, and yet, in Mr. Lowell's words for another, yet a parallel case, I plead that "Poets are always entitled to a royalty on whatever we find in their works; for these fine creations as truly build themselves up in the brain as they are built up with deliberate thought." If a garden owed none of its characteristics to its maker, if it had not expressed the mind of its designer, why the essential differences of the garden of this style and of that! Properly speaking, the music of all gardens is framed out of the same simple gamut of Nature's notes—it is but one music poured from myriad lips—yet out of the use of the same raw elements what a variety of tunes can be made, each tune complete in itself! And it is because we may identify the maker in his work; because, like the unfinished air, abruptly brought to a close at the master's death, the place is much as it was first schemed, one is jealous for the honour of the man whose eye prophesied its ultimate magic even as he initiated its plan, and drafted its lines.

Many an English house has been hopelessly

vulgarised and beggared by the banishment of the old pleasaunces of the days of Elizabeth, or of the Jameses and Charleses, and their wholesale demolition there and then struck a blow at English gardening from which it has not yet recovered. It may be admitted that, in the case of an individual garden here and there, the violation of these relics may be condoned on the heathen principle of tit for tat, because Art had, in the first instance, so to speak, turned her back on some fair landscape that Providence had provided upon the site, preferring to focus man's eye *within* rather than *without* the garden's bounds, therefore the vengeance is merited. Yet, where change was desirable, it had been better to modify than to destroy.

> "Cut is the branch that might have grown full straight,
> And burned is Apollo's laurel bough."

Certain it is that along with the girdle of high hedge or wall has gone that air of inviting mystery and homely reserve that our forefathers loved, and which is to me one of the pleasantest traits of an old English garden, best described as

> "A haunt of ancient peace."

CHAPTER V.

THE "LANDSCAPE-GARDEN."

"'Pealing from Jove to Nature's bar
Bold Alteration pleades
Large evidence; but Nature soon
Her righteous doom areads."—SPENSER.

WHY were the old-fashioned gardens destroyed? Firstly, because the traditional garden of the early part of the eighteenth century, when the reaction set in, represented a style which had run to seed, and men were tired of it; secondly, because the taste for foreign trees and shrubs, that had existed for a long time previously, then came to a head, and it was found that the old type of garden was not fitted for the display of the augmented stock of foreign material. Here was a new element in garden-craft, a new chance of decoration in the way of local colours in planting, which required a new adjustment of garden-effects; and as there was some difficulty in accommodating the new and the old, the problem was met by the abolition of the old altogether.

As to this matter of the sudden increase of specimen plants, Loudon remarks that in the earlier century the taste for foreign plants was confined to a few, and they not wealthy persons; but in the eighteenth century the taste for planting foreign trees extended itself among rich landed proprietors. A host of amateurs, botanists, and commercial gardeners were busily engaged in enriching the British Arboretum, and the garden-grounds had to be arranged for new effects and a new mode of culture. In Loudon's "Arboretum" (p. 126) is a list of the species of foreign trees and shrubs introduced into England up to the year 1830. He calculates that the total number of specimens up to the time that he wrote was about 1,400, but the numbers taken by centuries are: in the sixteenth century, 89; in the seventeenth century, 131; in the eighteenth century, 445; and in the first three decades of the nineteenth century, 699!

Men stubbed up the old gardens because they had grown tired of their familiar types, as they tire of other familiar things. The eighteenth century was essentially a critical age, an age of enquiry, and gardening, along with art, morals, and religion, came in for its share of coffee-house discussion, and elaborate essay-writing, and nothing was considered satisfactory. As to gardening, it was not natural enough for the critics. The works of Salvator and Poussin had pictured the grand and terrible in scenery, Thomson was writing naturalistic poetry, Rousseau naturalistic prose. Garden-ornament was too classical and formal for the varnished *littérateur* of the *Spectator* and the *Guardian*—too symmetrical for the jingling rhymester of a sing-song generation—too artificial for the essayist "'Pealing from Jove to Nature's bar," albeit he is privately content to go on touching up his groves and grottoes at Twickenham, securing the services of a peer

> "To form his quincunx, and to rank his vines."

Gardens are looked upon as so much "copy" to the essayist. What affected tastes have these critics! What a confession of counterfeit love, of selfish literary interest in gardens is this of Addison's: "I think there are as many kinds of gardening as of poetry. Your makers of parterres and flower-gardens are epigrammatists and sonneteers in this art; contrivers of bowers and grottoes, treillages and cascades, are romance writers." How beside nature, beside garden-craft, are such pen-man's whimsies! "Nothing to the true pleasure of a garden," Bacon would say.

Walpole's essay on gardening is entertaining reading, and his book gives us glimpses of the country-seats of all the great ladies and gentlemen who had the good fortune to be his acquaintances. His condemnation of the geometrical style of gardening common in his day, though quieter in tone than Pope's, was none the less effective in promoting a change of style. He tells how in Kip's views of the seats of our nobility we have the same "tiring and returning uniformity." Every house is approached by two or three gardens, consisting perhaps of a gravel-walk and two grass plats or borders of flowers. "Each rises above the other by two or three steps, and as many walks and terrasses; and so many iron gates, that we recollect those ancient romances in which every entrance was guarded by nymphs or dragons. At Lady Orford's, at Piddletown, in Dorsetshire, there was, when my brother married, a double enclosure of thirteen gardens, each, I suppose, not a hundred yards square, with an enfilade of correspondent gates; and before you arrived at these, you passed a narrow gut between two terrasses that rose above your head, and which were crowned by a line of pyramidal yews. A bowling-green was all the lawn admitted in those times, a circular lake the extent of magnificence."

Such an air of truth and soberness pervades Walpole's narrative, and to so absurd an extent has formality been manifestly carried under the auspices of Loudon and Wise, who had stocked our gardens with "giants, animals, monsters, coats of arms, mottoes in yew, box, and holly," that we are almost persuaded to be Vandals. "The compass and square, were of more use in plantations than the nursery-man. The measured walk, the quincunx, and the étoile imposed their unsatisfying sameness. . . . Trees were headed, and their sides pared away; many French groves seem green chests set upon poles. Seats of marble, arbours, and summer-houses, terminated every vista." It is all very well for Temple to recommend the regular form of garden. "I should hardly advise any of these attempts" cited by Walpole, "in the form of gardens among us; *they are adventures of too hard achievement for any common hands."* The truth will out! The "daintier sense" of garden-craft has vanished! According to Walpole, garden-adventure is to be henceforth journeyman's work, and Brown, the immortal kitchen-gardener, leads the way.

It were unfair to suspect that the exigencies of sprightly writing had carried Walpole beyond the bounds of accuracy in his description of the stiff-garden as he knew it, for things were in some respects very bad indeed. At the same time he is so engrossed with his abuse of old ways of gardening, and advocacy of the landscape-gardener's new-fangled notions, that his account of garden-craft generally falls short of completeness. He omits, for instance, to notice the progress in floriculture and horticulture of this time, the acquisitions being made in the ornamental foreign plants to be cultivated in the open ground, the green-house, and the stove. He omits to note that Loudon and Wise stocked our gardens with more than giants, animals, monsters, &c., in yew and box and holly. Because the names of these two worthies occur in this gardening text-book of Walpole's, all later essayists signal them out for blame. But Evelyn, who ranks as one of the three of England's great gardeners of old days, has a kindlier word for them. He is dilating upon the advantage to the gardener of the high clipped hedge as a protection for his shrubs and flowers, and goes on to particularise an oblong square, palisadoed with a hornbeam hedge "in that inexhaustible magazine at Brompton Park, cultivated by those two industrious fellow-gardeners,

Mr. Loudon and Mr. Wise." This hedge protects the orange trees, myrtles, and other rare perennials and exotics from the scorching rays of the sun; and it equally well shelters the flowers. "Here the Indian Narcissus, Tuberoses, Japan Lillies, Jasmines, Jonquills, Periclimena, Roses, Carnations, with all the pride of the parterre, intermixt between the tree-cases, flowery vases, busts, and statues, entertain the eye, and breathe their redolent odours and perfumes to the smell." Clearly there is an advantage in being a gardener if we write about gardens (provided you are not a mere "landscape-gardener!")

One cannot deny that Horace Walpole did well to expose the absurd vagaries which were being perpetrated about his time under Dutch influences. Close alliance with Holland through the House of Orange had affected every department of horticulture. True, it had enriched our gardens and conservatories with many rare and beautiful species of flowers and bulbs, and had imbued the English collector with the tulip-mania. So far good. But to the same source we trace the reign of the shears in the English garden, which made Art in a Garden ridiculous, and gave occasion to the enemy to blaspheme.

"The gardeners about London," says Mr. Lambert, writing to the Linnæan Transactions in 1712, "were remarkable for fine cut greens, and clipt yews in the shapes of birds, dogs, men, ships, &c. Mr. Parkinson in Lambeth was much noticed for these things, and he had besides a few myrtles, oleanders, and evergreens."

> "The old order changeth . . .
> Lest one good custom should corrupt the world."

And now is Art in a Garden become ridiculous. Since the beginning of things English gardeners had clipped and trimmed their shrubs; but had never carried the practice beyond a reasonable extent, and had combined it with woody and shady effects. With the onset of Dutch influence country-aspects vanish. Nature is reduced to a prosaic level. The traditional garden, whose past had been one long series of noble chances in fine company, now found content as the pedant's darling where it could have no opening for living romance, but must be tricked out in stage conventions, and dwindle more and more into a thing of shreds and patches!

Having arrived at such a pass, it was time that change should come, and change did come, with a vengeance! But let us not suppose that the change was from wrong to right. For, indeed, the revolution meant only that formality gone mad should be supplanted by informality gone equally mad. And we may note as a significant fact, that the point of departure is the destruction of the garden's boundaries, and the substitution of the ha-ha. It was not for the wild improvers to realise how Art that destroys its own boundaries is certainly doomed to soon have no country to boast of at all! It proved so in this case. From this moment, the very thought of garden-ornament was clean put out of mind, and the grass is carried up to the windows of the great house, as though the place were nothing better than a farm-shanty in the wilds of Westmoreland!

But to return to the inauguration of the "landscape-garden." The hour produced its men in Kent, and "the immortal Brown," as Repton calls him. Like many another "discovery," theirs was really due to an accident. Just as it was the closely-corked bottle that popped that gave birth to champagne, so it was only when our heroes casually leaped the ha-ha that they had made that they realised that all England outside was one vast rustic garden, from whence it were a shame to exclude anything!

So began the rage for making all the surroundings of a house assume a supposed appearance of rude Nature. Levelling, ploughing, stubbing-up, was the order of the day. The British navvy was in great request—in fact the day that Kent and Brown discovered England was this worthy's natal day. Artificial gardens must be demolished as impostures, and wriggling walks and turf put where they had stood. Avenues must be cut down or disregarded; the groves, the alleys, the formal beds, the terraces, the balustrades, the clipt hedges must be swept away as things intolerable. For the "landscape style" does not countenance a straight line, or terrace or architectural form, or symmetrical beds about the house; for to allow these would not be to photograph Nature. As carried into practice, the style demands that the house shall rise abruptly from the grass, and the general surface of the ground shall be characterised by smoothness and bareness (like Nature!) Hence in the grounds of this period, house and country

> "Wrapt all o'er in everlasting green
> Make one dull, vapid, smooth and tranquil scene."

There is to my mind no more significant testimony to the attractiveness and lovableness of the *regular* garden as opposed to the opened-out barbarism of the landscape-gardener's invention, than Horace Walpole's lament over the old gardens at Houghton,* which has the force of testimony wrung from unwilling lips :—

> "When I had drank tea I strolled into the garden. They told me it was now called the '*pleasure-ground.*' What a dissonant idea of pleasure! Those groves, those *alleys*, where I have passed so many charming moments, are now stripped up, or overgrown; many fond paths I could not unravel, though with a very exact clue in my memory. I met two gamekeepers and a thousand hares! In the days when all my soul was tuned to pleasure and vivacity, I hated Houghton and its solitude; *yet I loved this garden;* as now, with many regrets, I love Houghton ;—Houghton, I know not what to call it: a monument of grandeur or ruin!"—(Walpole's Letters.)

"What a dissonant idea of pleasure," this so-called 'pleasure-ground of the landscape-gardener!' "Those groves, those alleys where I have passed so many charming moments, stripped up! How I loved this garden!" Here is the biter bit, and it were to be more than human not to smile!

---

* Houghton was built by Sir R. Walpole, between 1722 and 1738. The garden was laid out in the stiff, formal manner by Eyre, "an imitator of Bridgman," and contained 23 acres. The park contains some fine old beeches. More than 1,000 cedars were blown down here in February, 1860.

With all the proper appliances at hand, it did not take long to transform the stiff garden into the barbaric. It did not take long to find out how *not* to do what civilisation had so long been learning how to do! The ancient "Geometric or Regular style" of garden—the garden of the aristocrat, with all its polished classicism—was to make way for the so-called "Naturalesque or Landscape style," and the garden of the *bourgeois*. Hope rose high in the breasts of the new professoriate. "A boon! a boon!" quoth the critic. And there is deep joy in navvydom. "Under the great leader, Brown," writes Repton ("Landscape Gardening," p. 327), "or rather those who patronised his discovery, we were taught that Nature was to be our only model." It was a grand moment. A Daniel had come to judgment! Nay, did not Brown "live to establish a fashion in gardening which might have been expected to endure as long as Nature should exist!"

The Landscape School of Gardeners, so-called, has been the theme of a great deal of literature, but with the exception of Walpole's and Addison's essays, and Pope's admirable chaff, very little has survived the interest it had at the moment of publication.

The other chief writers of this School, in its early phase, are George Mason, Whately,* Mason the

* Thomas Whately's "Observations on Modern Gardening," was published in 1770, fifteen years before Walpole's "Essay on Modern Gardening." Gilpin's book "On Picturesque Beauty," though published in part in 1782, belongs really to the second phase of the Landscape School. Shenstone's "Unconnected Thoughts on the Garden" was published in 1764, and is written pretty much from the standpoint of Kent. "An Essay on Design in Gardening," by G. Mason, was published in 1795.

poet, and Shenstone, our moon-struck friend quoted above, with his "assignation seats with proper mottoes, urns to faithful lovers," &c. Dr. Johnson did not think much of Shenstone's contributions to gardening :

> " He began from this time to point his prospects, to diversify his surface, to entangle his walks, and to wind his waters, which he did with such judgement and such fancy as made his little domain the envy of the great and the admiration of the skilful—a place to be visited by travellers and *copied by designers*. Whether to plant a walk in undulating curves, and to place a bench at every turn where there is an object to catch the view, to make water run where it will be heard, and to stagnate where it will be seen; to leave intervals where the eye will be pleased, and to thicken the plantation where there is something to be hidden—demand any great powers of the mind, I will not enquire ; perhaps a surly and sullen spectator may think such performances rather the sport than the business of human reason."—(Dr. Johnson, " Lives of the Poets," Shenstone.)

Whately's " Observations on Modern Gardening," published 1770, are well written and distinctly valuable as bearing upon the historical side of the subject. It says little for his idea of the value of Art in a garden, or of the function of a garden as a refining influence in life, to find Whately recommending " a plain field or a sheep-walk " as part of a garden's embellishments—" as an agreeable relief, and even wilder scenes."

But what astounds one more is, that a writer of Whately's calibre can describe Kent's gardens at Stowe, considered to be his masterpiece, as a sample of the non-formality of the landscape-gardener's Art, while he takes elaborate pains to show that it is full of would-be artistic subterfuges in Nature, full of architectural shams throughout. These gardens were begun by Bridgman, "Begun," Whately says, " when regularity was in fashion ; and the original boundary is still preserved on account of its magnificence, for round the whole circuit, of between three and four miles, is carried a very broad gravel-walk, planted with rows of trees, and open either to the park or the country ; a deep sunk-fence attends it all the way, and comprehends a space of near 400 acres. But in the interior spaces of the garden few traces of regularity appear ; where it yet remains in the plantations it is generally disguised ; every symptom almost of formality is obliterated from the ground ; and an octagon basin at the bottom is now converted into an irregular piece of water, which receives on one hand two beautiful streams, and falls on the other down a cascade into a lake."

And then follows a list of sham architectural features that are combined with sham views and prospects to match. "The whole space is divided into a number of scenes, each distinguished with taste and fancy ; and the changes are so frequent, so sudden and complete, the transitions so artfully conducted, that the ideas are never continued or repeated to satiety." In the front of the house two elegant Doric pavilions. On the brow of some rising grounds a Corinthian arch. On a little knoll an open Ionic rotunda—an Egyptian pyramid stands on its brow ; the Queen's Pillar in a recess on the descent, the King's Pillar elsewhere ; all the three buildings mentioned are "peculiarly adapted to a garden scene." In front of a wood three pavilions joined by arcades, all of the Ionic order, "characteristically proper for a garden, and so purely ornamental." Then a Temple of Bacchus, the Elysian fields, British remains; misshaped elms and ragged firs are frequent in a scene of solitude and gloom, which the trunks of dead trees assist. Then a large Gothic building, with slated roofs, "in a noble confusion"; then the Elysian fields, seen from the other side, a Palladian bridge, Doric porticoes, &c., the whole thing finished off with the Temple of Concord and Victory, probably meant as a not-undeserved compliment to the successfully chaotic skill of the landscape-gardener, who is nothing if not irregular, natural, non-formal, non-fantastical, non-artificial, and non-geometrical.

Two other points about Whately puzzle me. How comes he to strain at the gnat of formality in the old-fashioned garden, yet readily swallow the camel at Stowe? How can he harmonise his appreciation of the elaborately contrived and painfully assorted shams at Stowe, with his recommendation of a sheep-walk in your garden "as an agreeable relief, and even wilder scenes"?

Whether the beauty of the general disposition of the ground at Stowe is to be attributed to Kent or to Bridgman, who began the work, as Whately says, "when regularity was in fashion," I cannot say. It is right to observe, however, that the prevailing characteristic of Kent's and Brown's landscapes was their smooth and bald surface. "Why this art has been called 'landscape-gardening,'" says the plain-spoken Repton, "perhaps he who gave it the title may explain. I can see no reason, unless it be the efficacy which it has shown in destroying landscapes, in which, indeed, it seems infallible." (Repton, p. 355.) "Our virtuosi," said Sir William Chambers, "have scarcely left an acre of shade, or three trees growing in a line from the Land's End to the Tweed."

It did not take the wiser spirits long to realise that Nature left alone was more natural. And this same Repton, who began by praising "the great leader Brown," has to confess again and again that, so far as results go, he is mistaken. The ground, he laments, must be everlastingly moved and altered. "One of the greatest difficulties I have experienced in practice proceeds from that fondness for levelling so prevalent in all Brown's workmen; every hillock is by them lowered, and every hollow filled, to produce a level surface." (Repton, p. 342.) Or again (p. 347): "There is something so fascinating in the appearance of water, that Mr. Brown thought it carried its own excuse, however unnatural the situation; and therefore, in many places, under his direction, I have found water, on the tops of the hills, which I have been obliged to remove into lower ground *because the deception was not sufficiently complete to satisfy the mind as well as the eye.*" Indeed, in this matter of levelling, Brown's system does not, on the face of it, differ from Le Nôtre's, where the natural contour of the landscape was not of much account; or rather, it was thought the better if it had no natural contour at all, but presented a flat plain or plateau with no excrescences to interfere with the designer's schemes.

So much, then, for the pastoral simplicity of Nature edited by the "landscape-gardener." And let us note that under the auspices of the new *régime*, not only is Nature to be changed, but changed more than was ever dreamt of before; the transformation shall at once be more determined in its character and more deceptive than had previously been attempted. We were to have an artistically natural world, not a naturally artistic one; the face of the landscape was to be purged of its modern look and made to look primæval. And in this doing, or undoing, of things, the only art that was to be admitted was the art of consummate deceit, which shall "satisfy the mind as well as the eye." Yet call the man pope or presbyter, and beneath his clothes he is the same man! There is not a pin to choose as regards artificiality in the *aims* of the two schools, only in the *results*. The naked or *undressed* garden has studied irregularity, while the *dressed* garden has studied regularity and style. The first has, perhaps, an excessive regard for expression, the other has an emphatic scorn for expression. One garden has its plotted levels, its avenues, its vistas, its sweeping lawns, its terraces, its balustrades, colonnades, geometrical beds, gilded temples, and sometimes its fountains that won't play, and its fine vases full of nothing! The other begins with fetching back the chaos of a former world, and has for its category of effects, sham primævalisms, exaggerated wildness, tortured levellings, cascades, rocks, dead trunks of trees, ruined castles, lakes on the tops of hills, and sheep-runs hard by your windows. One school cannot keep the snip of the scissors off tree and shrub, the other mimics Nature's fortuitous wildness in proof of his disdain for the white lies of Art.

And all goes to show, does it not? that inasmuch as the art of gardening implies craft, and as man's imitation of Nature is bound to be unlike Nature, it were wise to be frankly inventive in gardening on Art lines. Success may attend one's efforts in the direction of Art, but in the direction of Nature, never.

The smooth, bare, and almost bald appearance which characterises Brown and Kent's school fails to satisfy for long, and there springs up another school which deals largely in picturesque elements, and rough intricate effects. The principles of the "Picturesque School," as it was called, are to be found in the writings of the Rev. William Gilpin and Sir Uvedale Price. Their books are full of careful observations upon the general composition of landscape-scenery, and what was then called "Landscape Architecture," as though every English building of older days that was worth a glance had not been "Landscape Architecture" fit for its site! Gilpin's writings contain an admirable discourse upon

"Forest Scenery," well illustrated. This work is in eight volumes, in part published in 1782, and it consists mainly in an account of the author's tours in every part of Great Britain, with a running commentary on the beauties of the scenery, and a description of the important country seats he passed on the way. Price helped by his writings to stay the rage for destroying avenues and terraces, and we note that he is fully alive to the necessity of uniting a country-house with the surrounding scenery by architectural adjuncts.

The taste for picturesque gardening was doubtless helped by the growing taste for landscape painting, exhibited in the works of the school of Wilson and Gainsborough, and in the pastoral writings of Thomson, Crabbe, Cowper, and Gray. It would farther be accelerated, as we suggested at the outset of this chapter, by the large importation of foreign plants and shrubs now going on.

What is known as the Picturesque School soon had for its main exponent Repton. He was a genius in his way—a born gardener,* able and thoughtful in his treatments, and distinguished among his fellows by a broad and comprehensive grasp of the whole character and surroundings of a site, in reference to the general section of the land, the style of the house to which his garden was allied, and the objects for which it was to be used. The sterling quality of his

---

* Loudon calls this School "Repton's," the "*Gardenesque*" School, its characteristic feature being "the display of the beauty of trees and other plants *individually*."

writings did much to clear the air of the vapourings of the critics who had gone before him, and his practice, founded as it was upon sound principles, redeemed the absurdities of the earlier phase of his school and preserved others from further development of the silly rusticities upon which their mind seemed bent. Although some of his ideas may now be thought pedantic and antiquated, the books which contain them will not die. Passages like the following mark the man and his aims: "I do not profess to follow Le Nôtre or Brown, but, selecting beauties from the style of each, to adopt so much of the grandeur of the former as may accord with a palace, and so much of the grace of the latter as may call forth the charms of natural landscape. Each has its proper situation; and good taste will make fashion subservient to good sense" (p. 234). "In the rage for picturesque beauty, let us remember that the landscape holds an inferior rank to the historical picture; one represents nature, the other relates to man in a state of society" (p. 236).

Repton sums up the whole of his teaching in the preface to his "Theory and Practice of Landscape Gardening" under the form of objections to prevailing errors, and they are so admirable that I cannot serve the purposes of my book better than to insert them here.

Objection No. 1. "There is no error more prevalent in modern gardening, or more frequently carried to excess, than taking away hedges to unite many small fields into one extensive and naked lawn, before plantations are made to give it the appearance of a park; and where ground is subdivided by sunk fences, imaginary freedom is dearly purchased at the expense of actual confinement."

No. 2. "The baldness and nakedness round the house is part of the same mistaken system, of concealing fences to gain extent. A palace, or even an elegant villa, in a grass field, appears to me incongruous; *yet I have seldom had sufficient influence to correct this common error.*"

No. 3. "An approach which does not evidently lead to the house, or which does not take the shortest course, cannot be right. (This rule must be taken with certain limitations.) The shortest road across a lawn to a house will seldom be found graceful, and often vulgar. A road bordered by trees in the form of an avenue may be straight without being vulgar; and grandeur, not grace or elegance, is the expression expected to be produced."

No. 4. "A poor man's cottage, divided into what is called a *pair of lodges*, is a mistaken expedient to mark importance in the entrance to a park."

No. 5. "The entrance-gate should not be visible from the mansion, unless it opens into a courtyard."

No. 6. "The plantation surrounding a place called a *Belt* I have never advised; nor have I ever willingly marked a drive, or walk, completely round the verge of a park, except in small villas, where a dry path round a person's own field is always more interesting than any other walk."

No. 7. "Small plantations of trees, surrounded by a fence, are the best expedients to form groups, because trees planted singly seldom grow well; neglect of thinning and removing the fence has produced that ugly deformity called a *Clump*."

No. 8. "Water on an eminence, or on the side of a hill, is among the most common errors of Mr. Brown's followers; in numerous instances I have been allowed to remove such pieces of water from the hills to the valleys, but in many my advice has not prevailed."

No. 9. "Deception may be allowable in imitating the works of Nature. Thus artificial rivers, lakes, and rock scenery can only be great by deception, and the mind acquiesces in the fraud after it is detected, but in works of Art every trick ought to be avoided. Sham churches, sham ruins, sham bridges, and everything which appears what it is not, disgusts when the trick is discovered."

No. 10. "In buildings of every kind the *character* should be strictly observed. No incongruous mixture can be justified. To add Grecian to Gothic, or Gothic to Grecian, is equally absurd; and a sharp pointed arch to a garden gate or a dairy window, however frequently it occurs, is not less offensive than Grecian architecture, in which the standard rules of relative proportion are neglected or violated."

The perfection of landscape-gardening consists

in the fullest attention to these principles, *Utility, Proportion,* and *Unity,* or harmony of parts to the whole. (Repton, "Landscape Gardening," pp. 128-9.)

The best advice one can give to a young gardener is—*know your Repton.*

The writings of the new school of gardening, of which Repton is a notable personage in its later phase, are not, however, on a par with the writings of the old traditional school, either as pleasant garden literature, or in regard to broad human interest or artistic quality. They are hard and critical, and never lose the savour of the heated air of controversy in which they were penned. Indeed, I can think of no more sure and certain cure for a bad attack of garden-mania—nothing that will sooner wipe the bloom off your enjoyment of natural beauty—than a course of reading from the Classics of Landscape-garden literature! "I only sound the clarion," said the urbane master-gardener of an earlier day, "but I enter not into the battle." But these are at one another's throats! Who enters here must leave his dreams of fine gardening behind, for he will find himself in a chilly, disenchanted world, with nothing more romantic to feed his imagination upon than "Remarks on the genius of the late Mr. Brown," Critical enquiries, Observations on taste, Difference between landscape gardening and painting, Price upon Repton, Repton upon Price, Repton upon Knight, further answers to Messrs. Price and Knight, &c. But all this is desperately dull reading, hurt-

ful to one's imagination, fatal to garden-fervour.*
And naturally so, for analysis of the processes of
garden-craft carried too far begets loss of faith in all.
Analysis is a kill-joy, destructive of dreams of beauty.
"We murder to dissect." That was a true word of
the cynic of that day, who summed up current controversy upon gardening in the opinion that "the
works of Nature were well executed, but in a bad
taste." The quidnuncs' books about gardening are
about as much calculated to give one delight, as the
music the child gets out of the strings of an instrument that it broke for the pride of dissection. Even
Addison, with the daintiest sense and prettiest pen
of them all, shows how thoroughly gardening had
lost

>. . . . "its happy, country tone,
>Lost it too soon, and learnt a stormy note
>Of men contention-tost,"—

as he thrums out his laboured coffee-house conceit.
"I think there are as many kinds of gardening as
poetry; your makers of parterres and flower-
gardens are epigrammatists and sonneteers in this
art; contrivers of bowers and grottoes, treillages, and
cascades, are romance writers. Wise and Loudon
are our heroic poets." Nor is his elaborate argument meant to prove the gross inferiority of Art in a

---

* A candid friend thus writes to Repton: "You may have per-
ceived that I am rather *too much* inclined to the Price and Knight
party, and yet I own to you that I have been often so much disgusted
by the affected and technical language of connoisseurship, that I have
been sick of pictures for a month, and almost of Nature, when the
same jargon was applied to her." (Repton, p. 232.)

garden to unadorned Nature more inspiring. Nay, what is one to make of even the logic of such argument as this? "If the products of Nature rise in value according as they more or less resemble those of Art, we may be sure that artificial works receive a greater advantage from their resemblance of such as are natural." (*Spectator*.) But who *does* apply the Art-standard to Nature, or value her products as they resemble those of Art? And has not Sir Walter well said: "Nothing is more the child of Art than a garden"? And Loudon: "All art, to be acknowledged, as art must be avowed."

One prefers to this cold Pindaric garden-homage the unaffected, direct delight in the sweets of a garden of an earlier day; to realise with old Mountaine how your garden shall produce "a jucunditie of minde;" to think with Bishop Hall, as he gazes at his tulips, "These Flowers are the true Clients of the Sunne;" to be brought to old Lawson's state of simple ravishment, "What more delightsome than an infinite varietie of sweet-smelling flowers? decking with sundry colours the green mantle of the Earth, colouring not onely the earth, but decking the ayre, and sweetning every breath and spirit;" to taste the joys of living as, taking Robert Burton's hand, you "walk amongst orchards, gardens, bowers, mounts and arbours, artificial wildernesses, green thickets, groves, lawns, rivulets, fountains, and such like pleasant places, between wood and water, in a fair meadow, by a river side, to disport in some pleasant plain or park, must needs be a delectable recreation;"

to be inoculated with old Gerarde of the garden-mania as he bursts forth, "Go forwarde in the name of God: graffe, set, plant, nourishe up trees in every corner of your grounde;" to trace with Temple the lines and features that go to make the witchery of the garden at Moor Park, "in all kinds the most beautiful and perfect, at least in the Figure and Disposition, that I have ever seen," and which you may follow if you are not "above the Regards of Common Expence;" to hearken to Bacon expatiate upon the Art which is indeed "the purest of all humane pleasure, the greatest refreshment to the Spirits of man;" to feel in what he says the value of an ideal, the magic of a style backed by passion—to have garden precepts wrapped in pretty metaphors (such as that "because the Breath of Flowers is far Sweeter in the Air—*where it comes and goes like the warbling of Musick*—than in the Hand, therefore nothing is more fit for that Delight than to know what be the Flowers and Plants that do best perfume the Air;")—to be taught how to order a garden to suit all the months of the year, and have the things of beauty enumerated according to their seasons—to feel rapture at the sweet-breathing presence of Art in a garden—to learn from one who knows how to garden in a grand manner, and yet be finally assured that beauty does not require a great stage, that the things thrown in "for state and magnificence" are but nothing to the true pleasure of a garden—this is garden-literature worth reading!

Compared with the frank raptures of such

writings as these, the laboured treatises of the landscape-school are but petty hagglings over the mint and cummin of things. You go to the writings of the masters of the old formality, to come away invigorated as by a whiff of mountain air straight off Helicon; they shall give one fresh enthusiasm for Nature, fresh devotion to Art, fresh love for beautiful things. But from the other—

"The bloom is gone, and with the bloom go I"—

they deal with technicalities in the affected language of connoisseurship; they reveal a disenchanted world, a world of exploded hopes given over to the navvies and the critics; and it is no wonder that writings so prompted should have no charm for posterity; charm they never had. They are dry as summer dust.

For the honour of English gardening, and before closing this chapter, I would like to recall that betweenity—the garden of the transition—done at the very beginning of the century of revolution, which unites something of the spirit of the old and of the new schools. Here is Sir Walter Scott's report of the Kelso garden as he *first* knew it, and *after* it had been mauled by the landscape-gardener. It was a garden of seven or eight acres adjacent to the house of an ancient maiden lady:

"It was full of long straight walks between hedges of yew and hornbeam, which rose tall and close on every side. There were thickets of flowering shrubs, a bower, and an arbour, to which access was obtained through a little maze of contorted walks, calling itself a labyrinth. In the centre of the bower was a splendid Platanus or Oriental plane, a huge hill of leaves, one of the noblest specimens of that regularly beautiful tree which we remember to have seen. In different parts of the garden were fine ornamental trees which had attained great size, and the orchard was filled with fruit-trees of the best description. There were seats and trellis-walks, and a banqueting-house. Even in our time this little scene, intended to present a formal exhibition of vegetable beauty, was going fast to decay. The parterres of flowers were no longer watched by the quiet and simple *friends* under whose auspices they had been planted, and much of the ornament of the domain had been neglected or destroyed to increase its productive value. We visited it lately, after an absence of many years. Its air of retreat, the seclusion which its alleys afforded was gone ; the huge Platanus had died, like most of its kind, in the beginning of this century ; the hedges were cut down, the trees stubbed up, and the whole character of the place so much destroyed that I was glad when I could leave it."—(" Essay on Landscape Gardening," *Quarterly Review*, 1828.*)

Another garden, of later date than this at Kelso, and somewhat less artistic, is that described by Mr. Henry A. Bright in " The English Flower Garden."†

"One of the most beautiful gardens I ever knew depended almost entirely on the arrangement of its lawns and shrubberies. It had certainly been most carefully and adroitly planned, and it had every advantage in the soft climate of the West of England. The various lawns were divided by thick shrubberies, so that you wandered on from one to the other, and always came on something new. In front of these shrubberies was a large margin of flower-border, gay with the most effective plants and annuals. At the corner of the lawn a standard *Magnolia grandiflora* of great size held up its chaliced blossoms ; at another a tulip-tree was laden with hundreds of yellow flowers. Here a magnificent *Salisburia* mocked the foliage of the maiden-hair ; and here an old cedar swept the grass with its large pendent branches. But the main breadth of each lawn was never destroyed, and past them you might see the reaches of a river, now in one aspect, now in another. Each view was different, and each was a fresh enjoyment and surprise.

"A few years ago and I revisited the place ; the 'improver' had been at work, and had been good enough to *open up* the view. Shrubberies had disappeared, and lawns had been thrown together. The pretty peeps among the trees were gone, the long vistas had become open spaces, and you saw at a glance all that there was to be seen.

* " The Praise of Gardens," pp. 185-6.
† *Ibid.*, p. 296.

Of course the herbaceous borders, which once contained numberless rare and interesting plants, had disappeared, and the lawn in front of the house was cut up into little beds of red pelargoniums, yellow calceolarias, and the rest."

In this example we miss the condensed beauty and sweet austerities of the older garden at Kelso; nevertheless, it represents a phase of workmanship which, for its real insight into the secrets of garden-beauty, we may well be proud of, and deplore its destruction at the hands of the landscape-gardener.

All arts are necessarily subject to progression of type. "Man cannot escape from his time," says Mr. Morley, and with changed times come changed influences. But, then, to *progress* is not to *change:* "to progress is to live," and one phase of healthy progression will tread the heels of that which precedes it. The restless changeful methods of modern gardening are, however, not to be ascribed to the healthy development of one consistent movement, but to chaos—to the revolution that ensued upon the overthrow of tradition—to the indeterminateness of men who have no guiding principles, who take so many wild leaps in the dark, in the course of which, rival champions jostle one another and only the fittest survives.

In treating of Modern English Gardening, it is difficult to make our way along the tortuous path of change, development it is not, that set in with the banishment of Art in a garden. Critical writers have done their best to unravel things, to find the relation of each fractured phase, and to give each phase a descriptive name, but there are still many unexplained points, many contradictions that are unsolved, to which I have already alluded.

Loudon's Introduction to Repton's " Landscape Gardening" gives perhaps the most intelligible account of the whole matter. The art of laying out grounds has been displayed in two very distinct styles: the first of which is called the " Ancient Roman, Geometric, Regular, or Architectural Style; and the second the Modern; *English*,* Irregular, Natural, or Landscape Style."

We have, he says, the Italian, the French, and the Dutch Schools of the Geometric Style. The Modern, or Landscape Style, when it first displayed itself in English country residences, was distinctly marked by the absence of everything that had the appearance of a terrace, or of architectural forms, or lines, immediately about the house. The house, in short, rose abruptly from the lawn, and the general surface of the ground was characterised by smoothness and bareness. This constituted the first School of the Landscape Style, introduced by Kent and Brown.

This manner was followed by the romantic or Picturesque Style, which inaugurates a School which aimed at producing architectural tricks and devices, allied with scenery of picturesque character and sham rusticity. The conglomeration at Stowe, albeit that it is attributed to Kent, shows what man can do in the way of heroically wrong garden-craft.

* This is a little unpatriotic of Loudon to imply that the *English* had no garden-style till the 18th century, but one can stand a great deal from Loudon.

To know truly how to lay out a garden "*After a more Grand and Rural Manner than has been done before,*" you cannot do better than get Batty Langley's "New Principles of Gardening," and among other things you have rules whereby you may concoct natural extravagances, how you shall prime prospects, make landscapes that are pictures of nothing and very like; how to copy hills, valleys, dales, purling streams, rocks, ruins, grottoes, precipices, amphitheatres, &c.

The writings of Gilpin and Price were effective in undermining Kent's School; they helped to check the rage for destroying avenues and terraces, and insisted upon the propriety of uniting a country-house with the surrounding scenery by architectural appendages. The leakage from the ranks of Kent's School was not all towards the Picturesque School, but to what Loudon terms Repton's School, which may be considered as combining all that was excellent in what had gone before.

Following upon these phases is one that is oddly called the "*Gardenesque*" Style, the leading feature of which is that it illustrates the beauty of trees, and other plants *individually ;* in short, it is the *specimen* style. According to the practice of all previous phases of modern gardening, trees, shrubs, and flowers were indiscriminately mixed and crowded together, in shrubberies or other plantations. According to the Gardenesque School, all the trees and shrubs are arranged to suit their kinds and dimensions, and to display them to advantage. The ablest exponents of the school are Loudon in the recent past, and Messrs. Marnock and Robinson in the present, and their method is based upon Loudon.

To know how to lay out a garden after the most approved modern fashion we have but to turn to the deservedly popular pages of "The English Flower Garden." This book contains not only model designs and commended examples from various existing gardens, but text contributed by some seventy professional and amateur gardeners. Even the gardener who has other ideals and larger ambitions than are here expected, heartily welcomes a book so well stored with modern garden-lore up to date, with suggestions for new aspects of vegetation, new renderings of plant life, and must earnestly desire to see any system of gardening made perfect after its kind—

    . . . . "I wish the sun should shine
    On all men's fruits and flowers, as well as mine."

Gardening is, above all things, a progressive Art which has never had so fine a time to display its possibilities as now, if we were only wise enough to freely employ old experiences and modern opportunities. People are, however, so readily content with their stereotyped models, with barren imitations, with their petty list of specimens, when instead of half-a-dozen kinds of plants, their garden has room for hundreds of different plants of fine form—hardy or half-hardy, annual and bulbous—which would equally well suit the British garden and add to its wealth of beauty by varied colourings in spring, summer, and autumn. At present "the choke-muddle shrubbery, in which the poor flowering shrubs dwindle and kill each other, generally supports a few ill-grown and ill-chosen plants, but it is mainly distinguished for wide patches of bare earth in summer, over which, in better hands, pretty green things might crowd." The specimen plant has no chance of displaying itself under such conditions.

Into so nice a subject as the practice of Landscape-gardening of the present day it is not my intention to enter in detail, and for two good reasons. In the first place, the doctrines of a sect are best known by the writings of its representatives; and in this case, happily, both writings and representatives are plentiful. Secondly, I do not see that there is much to chronicle. Landscape-gardening is, in a sense, still in its fumbling stage; it has not increased its resources, or done anything heroic, even on wrong lines; it has not advanced towards any permanent, definable system of ornamentation since it began its gyrations in the last century. Its rival champions still beat the air. Even Repton was better off than the men of to-day, for he had, at least, his Protestant formulary of Ten Objections to swear by, which "mark those errors or absurdities in modern gardening and architecture to which I have never willingly subscribed" (p. 127 "Theory and Practice of Landscape-Gardening," 1803, quoted in full above).

But the present race of landscape-gardeners are, it strikes me, as much at sea as ever. True they threw up traditional methods as unworthy, but they had not learnt their own Art according to Nature before they began to practise it; and they are still in the throes of education. Their intentions are admirable beyond telling, but their work exhibits in the grossest forms the very vices they condemn in the contrary school; for the expression of their ideas is self-conscious, strained, and pointless. To know at a glance their position towards Art in a garden, how crippled their resources, how powerless to design, let me give an extract from Mr. Robinson. He is speaking of an old-fashioned garden, "One of those classical gardens, the planners of which prided themselves upon being able to give Nature lessons of good behaviour, to teach her geometry and the fine Art of irreproachable lines; but Nature abhors lines;* she is for geometers a reluctant pupil, and if she submits to their tyranny she does it with bad grace, and with the firm resolve to take eventually her revenge. Man cannot conquer the wildness of her disposition, and so soon as he is no longer at hand to impose his will, so soon as he relaxes his care, she destroys his work" (p. viii., "English Flower Garden"). This is indeed to concede everything to Nature, to deny altogether the mission of Art in a garden.

* For which reason, I suppose, Mr. Robinson, in his model "Non-geometrical Gardens" (p. 5), humbly skirts his ground with a path which as nearly represents a tortured horse-shoe as Nature would permit; and his trees he puts in a happy-go-lucky-way, and allows them to nearly obliterate his path at their own sweet will! No wonder he does not fear Nature's revenge, where is so little Art to destroy!

K

And even the School that is rather kinder to Art, more lenient to tradition, represented by Mr. Milner—even he, in his admirable book upon the "Art and Practice of Landscape Gardening" (1890), is the champion of Nature, not of Art, in a garden. "Nature still seems to work in fetters," he says, and he would "form bases for a better practice of the Art" (p. 4). Again, "Nature is the great exemplar that I follow" (p. 8).

They have not got beyond Brown, so far as theory is concerned. "Under the great leader Brown," writes Repton, with unconscious irony, "or rather those who patronised his discovery, we were taught that Nature was to be our only model"—and Brown had his full chance of manipulating the universe, for "he lived to establish a fashion in gardening, which might have been expected to endure as long as Nature should exist"; and yet Repton's work mostly consisted in repairing Brown's errors and in covering the nakedness of his hungry prospects. So it would seem that Art has her revenges as well as Nature! "The way of transgressors is hard!"

The Landscape-gardener, I said, gets no nearer to maturity of purpose as time runs on. He creeps and shuffles after Nature as at the first—much as the benighted traveller after the will-o'-the-wisp. He may not lay hands on her, because you cannot conquer her wildness, nor impose your will upon her, or teach her good behaviour. He may not apply the "dead formalism of Art" to her, for

"Nature abhors lines." Hence his mimicry can never rise above Nature. Indeed, if it remains faithful to the negative opinions of its practitioners, landscape-gardening will never construct any system of device. It has no creed, if you except that sole article of its faith, " I believe in the non-geometrical garden." A monumental style is an impossibility while it eschews all features that make for state and magnificence and symmetry; a little park scenery, much grass, curved shrubberies, the " laboured littleness " of emphasised specimen plants —the hardy ones dotted about in various parts— wriggling paths, flower-borders, or beds of shapes that imply that they are the offspring of bad dreams, and its tale of effects is told. But as for " fine gardening," that was given up long ago as a bad job! The spirit of Walpole's objections to the heroic enterprise of the old-fashioned garden still holds the " landscape-gardener" in check. " I should hardly advise any of those attempts," says Walpole ; "*they are adventures of too hard achievement for any common hands.*"

It is not so much at what he finds in the landscape-gardener's creations that the architect demurs, but at what he misses. It is not so much at what the landscape-gardener recommends that the architect objects, as at what moving in his own little orbit he wilfully shuts out, basing his opposition to tradition upon such an *ex parte* view of the matter as this —" There are really two styles, one straitlaced, mechanical, with much wall and stone, or it may be gravel, with much also of such geometry as the designer of wall-papers excels in—often poorer than that, with an immoderate supply of spouting water, and with trees in tubs as an accompaniment, and, perhaps, griffins and endless plaster-work, and sculpture of the poorer sort." Why "poorer"? "The other, with *right desire*, though *often awkwardly* (!) accepting Nature as a guide, and endeavouring to illustrate in our gardens, *so far as convenience and knowledge will permit*, her many treasures of the world of flowers." ("English Flower Garden"). How sweetly doth bunkum commend itself!

It is not that the architect is small-minded enough to cavil at the landscape-gardener's right to display his taste by his own methods, but that he strikes for the same right for himself. It is not that he would rob the landscape-gardener of the pleasure of expressing his own views as persuasively as he can, but that he resents that air of superiority which the other puts on as he bans the comely types and garnered sweetness of old England's garden, that he accents the proscription of the ways of interpreting Nature that have won the sanction of lovers of Art and Nature of all generations of our forefathers, and this from a School whose prerogative dates no farther back than the discovery of the well-meaning, clumsy, now dethroned kitchen-gardener, known a short century since as "the immortal Brown." There is no reviewer so keen as Time!

CHAPTER VI.

THE TECHNICS OF GARDENING.*

" Nothing is more the Child of Art than a Garden."
                                    SIR WALTER SCOTT.

" FOR every Garden," says Sir William Temple, "four things are to be provided—Flowers, Fruit, Shade, and Water, and whoever lays out a garden without these, must not pretend it in any perfection. Nature should not be forced; great sums may be thrown away without Effect or Honour, if there want sense in proportion to this." Briefly, the old master's charge is this : " Have common-sense ; follow Nature."

Following upon these lines, the gardener's first duty in laying out the grounds to a house is, to study the site, and not only that part of it upon which the house immediately stands, but the whole site, its aspect, character, soil, contour, sectional lines, trees, &c. Common-sense, Economy, Nature, Art, alike dictate this. There is an individual character to every plot of land, as to every human face in a crowd; and that man is not wise who, to suit

---

* These notes make no pretence either at originality or completeness. They represent gleanings from various sources, combined with personal observations on garden-craft from the architect's point of view.—J. D. S.

preferences for any given style of garden, or with a view to copying a design from another place, will ignore the characteristics of the site at his disposal.

Equally unwise will he be to follow that school of gardening that makes chaos before it sets about to make order. Features that are based upon, or that grow out of the natural formation of the ground, will not only look better than the created features, but be more to the credit of the gardener, if successful, and will save expense.

The ground throughout should be so handled that every natural good point, every tree, mound, declivity, stream, or quarry, or other chance feature, shall be turned to good account, and its consequence heightened, avoiding the error of giving the thing mock importance, by planting, digging, lowering declivities, raising prominences, planting dark-foliaged trees to intensify the receding parts, forming terraces on the slope, or adding other architectural features as may be advisable to connect the garden with the house which is its *raison d'être*, and the building with the landscape.

What folly to throw down undulations in order to produce a commonplace level, or to throw up hills, or make rocks, lakes, and waterfalls should the site happen to be level! What folly to make a standing piece of water imitate the curves of a winding river that has no existence, to throw a bridge over it near its termination, so as to close the vista and suggest the continuation of the water beyond! Nay, what need of artificial lakes at all if there be a running stream hard by?*

It is of the utmost importance that Art and Nature should be linked together, alike in the near neighbourhood of the house, and in its far prospect, so that the scene as it meets the eye, whether at a distance or near, should present a picture of a simple whole, in which each item should take its part without disturbing the individual expression of the ground.

To attain this result, it is essential that the ground immediately about the house should be devoted to symmetrical planning, and to distinctly ornamental treatment; and the symmetry should break away by easy stages from the dressed to the undressed parts, and so on to the open country, beginning with wilder effects upon the country-boundaries of the place, and more careful and intricate effects as the house is approached. Upon the attainment of this appearance of graduated formality much depends. One knows houses that are well enough in their way, that yet figure as absolute blots upon God's landscape, and that make a man writhe as at

---

* "All rational improvement of grounds is necessarily founded on a due attention to the CHARACTER and SITUATION of the place to be improved; the *former* teaches what is advisable, the *latter* what is possible to be done. The *situation* of a place always depends on Nature, which can only be assisted, but cannot be entirely changed, or greatly controlled by ART; but the *character* of a place is wholly dependent on ART; thus the house, the buildings, the gardens, the roads, the bridges, and every circumstance which marks the habitation of man must be artificial; and although in the works of art we may imitate the forms and graces of Nature, yet, to make them truly natural, always leads to absurdity" (Repton, p. 341).

false notes in music, and all because due regard has not been paid to this particular. By exercise of forethought in this matter, the house and garden would have been linked to the site, and the site to the landscape; as it is, you wish the house at Jericho!*

As the point of access to a house from the public road and the route to be taken afterwards not infrequently determines the position of the house upon the site, it may be well to speak of the Approach first. In planning the ground, care will be taken that the approach shall both look well of itself and afford convenient access to the house and its appurtenances, not forgetting the importance of giving to the visitor a pleasing impression of the house as he drives up.

---

* Not so thinks the author of "The English Flower Garden:"— "Imagine the effect of a well-built and fine old house, seen from the extremity of a wide lawn, with plenty of trees and shrubs on its outer parts, and nothing to impede the view of the house or its windows but a refreshing carpet of grass. If owners of parks were to consider this point fully, and, as they travel about, watch the effect of such lawns as remain to us, and compare them with what has been done by certain landscape-gardeners, there would shortly be, at many a country-seat, a rapid carting away of the terrace and all its adjuncts." Marry, this is sweeping! But Repton has some equally strong words condemning the very plan our Author recommends: "In the execution of my profession I have often experienced great difficulty and opposition in attempting to correct the false and mistaken taste for placing a large house in a naked grass field, without any apparent line of separation between the ground exposed to cattle and the ground annexed to the house, which I consider as peculiarly under the management of art.

"This line of separation being admitted, advantage may be easily taken to ornament the lawn with flowers and shrubs, and to attach to the mansion that scene of 'embellished neatness' usually called a pleasure-ground" (Repton, p. 213. See also No. 2 of Repton's "Objections," given on p. 116).

In Elizabethan and Jacobean times, the usual form of approach was the straight avenue, instances of which are still to be seen at Montacute, Brympton, and Burleigh.* The road points direct to the house, as evidence that in the minds of the old architects the house was, as it were, the pivot round which the attached territory and the garden in all its parts radiated; and the road ends, next the house, in a quadrangle or forecourt, which has either an open balustrade or high hedge, and in the centre of the court is a grass plot enlivened by statue or fountain or sundial. And it is worthy of note that they who prefer a road that winds to the very door of a house on the plea of its naturalness make a great mistake; they forget that the winding road is no whit less artificial than the straight one.

The choice of avenue or other type of approach will mainly depend upon the character and situation of the house, its style and quality. Repton truly observes that when generally adopted the avenue reduces all houses to the same landscape—" if looking up a straight line, between two green walls, deserves the name of a landscape." He states his objections to avenues thus—" If at the end of a long avenue be placed an obelisk or temple, or any other eye-trap, ignorance or childhood alone will be caught and pleased by it; the eye of taste or experience hates compulsion, and turns away with disgust from every artificial means of attracting its notice; for this

---

* As an instance of how much dignity a noble house may lose by a meanly-planned drive, I would mention Hatfield.

reason an avenue is most pleasing which, like that at Langley Park, climbs up a hill, and passing over the summit, leaves the fancy to conceive its termination."

The very dignity of an avenue seems to demand that there shall be something worthy of this procession of trees at its end, and if the house to which this feature is applied be unworthy, a sense of disappointment ensues. Provided, however, that the house be worthy of this dignity, and that its introduction does not mar the view, or dismember the ground, an avenue is both an artistic and convenient approach.

Should circumstances not admit of the use of an avenue, the drive should be as direct as may well be, and if curved, there should be some clear and obvious justification for the curve or divergence; it should be clear that the road is diverted to obtain a glimpse of open country that would otherwise be missed, or that a steep hill or awkward dip is thus avoided. The irregularity in the line of the road should not, however, be the occasion of any break in the gradient of the road, which should be continuously even throughout. In this matter of planning roads, common sense, as well as artistic sense, should be satisfied; there should be no straining after pompous effects. Except in cases where the house is near to the public road, the drive should not run parallel to the road for the mere sake of gaining a pretentious effect. Nor should the road overlook the garden, a point that touches the comfort both of residents and visitors; and for the same reason the entrance to the garden should not be from the drive, but from the house.

The gradient recommended by Mr. Milner,* to whose skilled experience I am indebted for many practical suggestions, is 1 in 14. The width of a drive is determined by the relative importance of the route. Thus, a drive to the principal entrance of the house should be from 14 to 18 ft., while that to the stables or offices 10 ft. Walks should not be less than 6 ft. wide. The width of a grand avenue should be 50 ft., and "the trees may be preferably Elm, Beech, Oak, Chestnut, and they should not be planted nearer in precession than 40 ft., unless they be planted at intervals of half that distance for the purpose of destroying alternate trees, as their growth makes the removal necessary."

The entrance-gates should not be visible from the mansion, Repton says, unless it opens into a courtyard. As to their position, the gates may be formed at the junction of two roads, or where a cross-road comes on to the main road, or where the gates are sufficiently back from the public road to allow a carriage to stand clear. The gates, as well as the lodge, should be at right angles to the drive, and belong to it, not to the public road. Where the house and estate are of moderate size, architectural, rather than "rustic," simplicity best suits the character of the lodge. It is desirable, remarks Mr. Milner, to place the entrance, if it can be managed,

---

* Milner's "Art and Practice of Landscape-Gardening," p. 13, 14.

at the foot of a hill or rise in the public road, and not part of the way up an ascent, or at the top of it.

If possible, the house should stand on a platform or terraced eminence, so as to give the appearance of being well above ground; or it should be on a knoll where a view may be had. The ground-level of the house should be of the right height to command the prospect. Should the architect be so fortunate as to obtain a site for his house where the ground rises steep and abrupt on one side of the house, he will get here a series of terraces, rock-gardens, a fernery, a rose-garden, &c. The ideal site for a house would have fine prospects to the south-east and to the south-west. "The principal approach should be on the north-western face, the offices on the north-eastern side, the stables and kitchen-garden beyond. The pleasure-gardens should be on the south-eastern aspect, with a continuation towards the east; the south-western face might be open to the park" (Milner).

If it can be avoided, the house should not be placed where the ground slopes towards it—a treatment which suggests water draining into it—but if this position be for some sufficient reason inevitable, or should it be an old house with this defect that we are called to treat, then a good space should be excavated, at least of the level of the house, with a terrace-wall at the far end, on the original level of the site at that particular point. And as to the rest of the ground, Repton's sound advice is, to plant up the heights so as to increase the effect of shelter and seclusion that the house naturally has, and introduce water, if available, at the low-level of the site. The air of seclusion that the low-lying situation gives to the house is thus intensified by crowning the heights with wood and setting water at the base of the slope.

The hanging-gardens at Clevedon Court afford a good example of what can be done by a judicious formation of ground where the house is situated near the base of a slope, and this example is none the less interesting for its general agreement with Lamb's " Blakesmoor "—its ample pleasure-garden " rising backwards from the house in triple terraces ; . . . the verdant quarters backwarder still, and stretching still beyond in old formality, the firry wilderness, the haunt of the squirrel and the day-long murmuring wood-pigeon, with that antique image in the centre."

Before dealing with the garden and its relation to the house it may be well to say a few words upon Planting. Trees are among the grandest and most ornamental effects of natural scenery; they help the charm of hill, plain, valley, and dale, and the changes in the colour of their foliage at the different seasons of the year give us perpetual delight. One of the most important elements in ornamental garden is the dividing up and diversifying a given area by plantations, by grouping of trees to form retired glades, open lawns, shaded alleys, and well-selected margins of woods; and, if this be skilfully done, an impression of variety and extent will be produced beyond the belief of the uninitiated who has seen the bare site before it was planted.

To speak generally, there should be no need of apology for applying the most subtle art in the disposal of trees and shrubs, and in the formation of the ground to receive them. "*All Art*," as Loudon truly says (speaking upon this very point), "*to be acknowledged as Art, must be avowed.*" This is the case in the fine arts—there is no attempt to conceal art in music, poetry, painting, or sculpture, none in architecture, and none in geometrical-gardening.

In modern landscape-gardening, practised as a fine art, many of the more important beauties and effects produced by the artist depend on the use he makes of foreign trees and shrubs; and, personally, one is ready to forgive Brown much of his vile vandalism in old-fashioned gardens for the use he makes of cedars, pines, planes, gleditschias, robinias, deciduous cypress, and all the foreign hardy trees and shrubs that were then to his hand.

Loudon—every inch a fine gardener, true lineal descendant of Bacon in the art of gardening—recommends in his "Arboretum" (pp. 11, 12) the heading down of large trees of common species, and the grafting upon them foreign species of the same genus, as is done in orchard fruit-trees. Hawthorn hedges, for instance, are common everywhere; why not graft some of the rare and beautiful sorts of tree thorns, and intersperse common thorns between them? There are between twenty and thirty beautiful species and varieties of thorn in our nurseries. Every gardener can graft and bud. Or why should not scarlet oak and scarlet acer be grafted on common species of these genera along the margins of woods and plantations?

In planting, the gardener has regard for character of foliage and tints, the nature of the soil, the undulations of ground and grouping, the amount of exposure. Small plantations of trees surrounded by a fence are the best expedients to form groups, says Repton, because trees planted singly seldom grow well. Good trees should not be encumbered by peddling bushes, but be treated as specimens, each having its separate mound. The mounds can be formed out of the hollowed pathways in the curves made between the groups. The dotting of trees over the ground or of specimen shrubs on a lawn is destructive of all breadth of effect. This is not to follow Nature, nor Art, for Art demands that each feature shall have relation to other features, and all to the general effect.

In planting trees the variety of height in their outline must be considered as much as the variety of their outline on plan; the prominent parts made high, the intervening bays kept low,* and this both in connection with the lie of the ground and the plant selected. Uniform curves, such as parts of circles or ovals, are not approved; better effects are obtained by forming long bays or recesses with forked

---

* "One deep recess, one bold prominence, has more effect than twenty little irregularities." "Every variety in the outline of a wood must be a *prominence* or a *recess*" (Repton, p. 182).

tongues breaking forward irregularly, the turf running into the bays. Trees may serve to frame a particular view and frame a picture; and when well led up to the horizon will enhance the imaginative effect of a place: a *beyond* in any view implies somewhere to explore.

All trees grow more luxuriantly in valleys than on the hills, and on this account the tendency of tree-growth is to neutralise the difference in the rise and fall of the ground and to bring the tops of the trees level. But the perfection of planting is to get an effect approximating as near as may be to the charming undulations of the Forest of Dean and the New Forest. Care will be taken, then, not to plant the fast-growing, or tall-growing trees in the low-ground, but on the higher points, and even to add to the irregularity by clothing the natural peaks with silver fir, whose tall heads will increase the sense of height. The limes, planes, and elms will be mostly kept to the higher ground, bunches of Scotch fir will be placed here and there, and oaks and beeches grouped together, while the lower ground will be occupied by maples, crabs, thorns, alders, &c. "Fringe the edges of your wood with lines of horse-chestnut," says Viscount Lymington in his delightful and valuable article on "Vert and Venery"—"a mass in spring of blossom, and in autumn of colour; and under these chestnuts, and in nooks and corners, thrust in some laburnum, that it may push its showers of gold out to the light and over the fence."

As to the nature of the soil, and degree of exposure suitable to different forest-trees, the writer just quoted holds that, for exposure to the wind inland, the best trees for all soils are the beech, the Austrian pine, and the Scotch fir.

For exposure in hedgerows, the best tree to plant ordinarily is the elm. For exposure to frost, the Insignis pine, which will not, however, stand the frosts of the valley, but prefers high ground. For exposure to smoke, undoubtedly the best tree is the Western plane. The sycamore will stand better than most trees the smoke and chemical works of manufacturing towns. For sea-exposure, the best trees to plant are the goat willow and pineaster. Among the low-growing shrubs which stand sea-exposure well are mentioned the sea-buckthorn, the snowberry, the evergreen barberry, and the German tamarisk; to which should be added the euonymus and the escallonia.

With regard to the nature of the soil, Lord Lymington says: "Strong clay produces the best oaks and the best silver fir. A deep loam is the most favourable soil for the growth of the Spanish chestnut and ash. The beech is the glorious weed of the chalk and down countries; the elm of the rich red sandstone valleys. Coniferous trees prefer land of a light sandy texture; . . . but as many desire to plant conifers on other soils, I would mention that the following among others will grow on most soils, chalk included: the *Abies excelsa, canadensis, magnifica, nobilis,* and *Pinsapo;* the *Pinus excelsa, insignis,* and *Laricio;* the *Cupressus Lawsoniana, erecta, viridis,* and *macrocarpa*; the *Salisburia adiantifolia*, and the *Wellingtonia*. The most fast-growing in England of conifers is the Douglas fir. . . It grows luxuriantly on the slopes of the hills, but will not stand exposure to the wind, and for that reason should always be planted in sheltered combes with other trees behind it.

"In moist and boggy land the spruce or the willow tribes succeed best.

"In high, poor, and very dry land, no tree thrives so well as the Scotch fir, the beech, and the sycamore."

Avoid the selfishness and false economy of planting an inferior class of fast-growing trees such as firs and larches and Lombardy poplars, on the ground that one would not live to get any pleasure out of woods of oaks and beech and chestnut. How frequently one sees tall, scraggy planes, or belts of naked, attenuated firs, where groups of oaks and elms and groves of chestnut might have stood with greater advantage.

Avoid the thoughtlessness and false economy of not thoroughly preparing the ground before planting. "Those that plant," says an old writer, "should make their ground fit for the trees before they set them, and not bury them in a hole like a dead dog; let them have good and fresh lodgings suitable to their quality, and good attendance also, to preserve them from their enemies till they are able to encounter them."

Avoid trees near a house; they tend to make it damp, and the garden which is near the house untidy. Writers upon planting have their own ideas as to the fitness of certain growths for a certain style of house. As regards the relation of trees to the house, if the building be of Gothic design with the piquant outline usual to the style, then trees of round shape form the best foil; if of Classic or Renascence design, then trees of vertical conic growth suit best. So, if the house be of stone, trees of dark foliage best meet the case; if of brick, trees of lighter foliage should prevail. As a backing to the horizontal line of a roof to an ordinary two-storey building, nothing looks better than the long stems of stone pines or Scotch firs; and pines are health-giving trees.

Never mark the outline of ground, nor the shape of groups of trees and shrubs with formal rows of bedding plants or other stiff edging, which is the almost universal practice of gardeners in the present day. This is a poor travesty of Bacon's garden, who only allows low things to grow naturally up to the edges.

From the artist's point of view, perhaps the most desirable quality to aim at in the distribution of garden space is that of breadth of effect—in other words, simplicity; and the larger the garden the more need does there seem for getting this quality. One may, in a manner, *toy* with a small garden. In the case of a large garden, where the owner in his greed for prettiness has carried things further than regulation-taste would allow, much may be done to subdue the assertiveness of a multiplicity of interesting objects by architectural adjuncts—broad terraces, well-defined lines, even a range of sentinel yews or clipt shrubs—things that are precise, grave, calm, and monotonous. Where such things are brought upon the scene, a certain spaciousness and amplitude of effect ensues as a matter of course.

One sees that the modern gardener, with his augmented list of specimen-plants of varied foliage, is far more apt to err in the direction of sensationalism than the gardener of old days who was exempt from many of our temptations. Add to this power of attaining sweetness and intricacy the artist's prone aspirations to work up to his lights and opportunities, and we have temptation which is seductiveness itself!

The garden at Highnam Court, dear to me for its signs and memories of my late accomplished friend, Mr. T. Gambier Parry, is the perfectest modern garden I have ever seen. But here, if there be a fault, it is that Art has been allowed to blossom too profusely. The attention of the visitor is never allowed to drop, but is ever kept on the stretch. You are throughout too much led by the master's cunning hand. Every known bit of garden-artifice, every white lie of Art, every known variety of choice tree or shrub, or trick of garden-arrangement is set forth there. But somehow each thing strikes you as a little vainglorious—too sensible of its own importance. We go about in a sort of pre-Raphaelite frame of mind, where each seemly and beauteous feature has so much to say for itself that, in the delightfulness of the details, we are apt to forget that it is the first business of any work of Art to be a unit. There is nothing of single specimen, or group of intermingled variety, or adroit vista that we may miss and not be a loser; the only drawback is that we see what we are expected to see, what everyone else sees. Here is greenery of every hue; every metallic tint of silver, gold, copper, bronze is there; and old and new favourites take hands, and we feel that it is perfect; but the things blush in their conscious beauty—every prospect is best seen "*there!*" England has few such beautiful gardens as Highnam, and it has all the pathos of the touch of "a vanished hand," and ideals that have wider range now.

As to this matter of scenic effects, it is of course only fair to remember that a garden is a place meant not only for broad vision, but for minute scrutiny; and, specially near the house, intricacy is permissible. Yet the counsels of perfection would tell the artist to eschew such prettiness and multiplied beauties as trench upon broad dignity. Sweetness is not good everywhere. Variations in plant-life that are over-enforced, like variations in music, may be inferior to the simple theme. A commonplace house, with well-disposed grounds, flower-beds in the right place, a well-planted lawn, may please longer than a fine pile where is ostentation and unrelieved artifice.

Of lawns. Everything in a garden, we have said, has its first original in primal Nature: a garden is made up of wild things that are tamed. The old masters fully realised this. They sucked out the honey of wild things without carrying refinement too far before they sipped it; and in garnering for their *House Beautiful* the rustic flavour is left so far as was compatible with the requirements of Art—" as much as may be to a natural wildness." And it were well for us to do the same in the treatment of a lawn, which is only the grassy, sun-chequered, woodland glade in, or between woods, in a wild country, idealised.

A lawn is one of the delights of man. The " Teutonic races "—says Mr. Charles Dudley Warner, in his large American way—" The Teutonic races all love turf; they emigrate in the line of its growth." Flower-beds breed cheerfulness, but they may at times be too gay for tired eyes and jaded minds; they may provoke admiration till they are provoking. But a garden-lawn is a vision of peace, and its tranquil grace is a boon of unspeakable value to people doomed to pass their working-hours in the hustle of city-life.

The question of planting and of lawn-making runs together, and Nature admonishes us how to set about this work. Every resource she offers should be met by the resources of Art: avoid what she avoids, accept and heighten what she gives. Nature in the wild avoids half-circles and ovals and uniform curves, and they are bad in the planted park, both for trees and greensward. Nature does not of herself dot the landscape over with spies sent out single-handed to show the nakedness of the land, but puts forth detachments that befriend each the other, the boldest and fittest first, in jagged outlines, leading the way, but not out of touch with the rest. And, since the modern landscape-gardener is nothing if not a naturalist, this is why one cannot see the consistency of so fine a master as Mr. Marnock, when he dots his lawns over with straggling specimens. (See the model garden, by Mr. Marnock in "The English Flower-Garden," p. xxi., described thus—" Here the foreground is a sloping lawn; the flowers are mostly arranged near the kitchen garden, partly shown to right; the hardy ones grouped and scattered in various positions near, or within good view of, the one bold walk which sweeps round the ground.")

A garden is ground knit up artistically; ground which has been the field of artistic enterprise; ground which expresses the feeling of beauty and which absorbs qualities which man has discovered in the woodland world. And the qualities in Nature which may well find room in a garden are peace, variety, animation. A good sweep of lawn is a peaceful object, but see that the view is not impeded with the modern's sprawling pell-mell beds. And in the anxiety to make the most of your ground, do not spoil a distant prospect. Remember, too, that a lawn requires a good depth of soil, or it will look parched in the hot weather.

And since a lawn is so delightful a thing, beware lest your admiration of it lead you to swamp your whole ground with grass even to carrying it up to the house itself. "Nothing is more a child of Art than a garden," says, Sir Walter, and he was competent to judge. If only out of compliment to your architect and to the formal angularities of his building, let the ground immediately about the house be of an ornamental dressed character.

Avoid the misplaced rusticity of the fashionable landscape-gardener, who with his Nebuchadnezzar tastes would turn everything into grass, would cart away the terrace and all its adjuncts, do away with all flowers, and "lawn your hundred good acres of wheat," as Repton says, if you will only let him, and if you have them.

In his devotion to grass, his eagerness to display the measure of his art in the curves of shrubberies and the arrangement of specimen plants that strut across your lawn or dot it over as the Sunday scholars do the croft when they come for their annual treat, he quite forgets the flowers—forgets the old intent of a garden as the House Beautiful of the civilised world—the place for nature-rapture, colour-pageantry, and sweet odours. " Here the foreground is a sloping lawn ; the *flowers are mostly arranged near the kitchen garden*." Anywhere, anywhere out of the way! Or if admitted at all into view of the house, it shall be with little limited privileges, and the stern injunction—

"If you speak you must not show your face,
Or if you show your face you must not speak."

So much for the garden-craft of the best modern landscape-gardener and its relation to flowers. If this be the garden of the "Gardenesque" style, as it is proudly called, I personally prefer the garden without the style.

CHAPTER VII.

THE TECHNICS OF GARDENING (*continued*).

" I cannot think Nature is so spent and decayed that she can bring forth nothing worth her former years. She is always the same, like herself; and when she collects her strength is abler still. Men are decayed, and studies; she is not."—BEN JONSON.

THE old-fashioned country house has, almost invariably, a garden that curtseys to the house, with its formal lines, its terraces, and beds of geometrical patterns.

But to the ordinary Landscape-gardener the terrace is as much anathema as the " Kist o' whistles " to the Scotch Puritan ! So able and distinguished a gardener as Mr. Robinson, while not absolutely forbidding any architectural acessories or geometrical arrangement, is for ever girding at them. The worst thing that can be done with a true garden, he says (" The English Flower Garden," p. ii), "is to introduce any feature which, unlike the materials of our world-designer, never changes. There are positions, it is true, where the *intrusion of architecture* and embankment into the garden is justifiable ; nay, now and then, even necessary."

If one is to promulgate opinions that shall run counter to the wisdom of the whole civilised world, it is, of course, well that they should be pronounced with the air of a Moses freshly come down from the Mount, with the tables of the law in his hands. And there is more of it. " There is no code of taste resting on any solid foundation which proves that garden or park should have any extensive stonework or geometrical arrangement. . . . Let us, then, use as few oil-cloth or carpet patterns and as little stonework as possible in our gardens. The style is in doubtful taste in climates and positions more suited to it than that of England, but he who would adopt it in the present day is an enemy to every true interest of the garden " (p. vi).

So much for the "deadly formalism" of an old-fashioned garden in our author's eyes! But, as Horace Walpole might say, "it is not peculiar to Mr. Robinson to think in that manner." It is the way of the landscape-gardener to monopolise to himself all the right principles of gardening; he is the angel of the garden who protects its true interests; all other moods than his are low, all figures other than his are symbols of errors, all dealings with Nature or with "the materials of our world-designer" other than his are spurious. For the colonies I can imagine no fitter doctrines than our author's, but not for an old land like ours, and for methods that have the approval of men like Bacon, Temple, More, Evelyn, Sir Joshua, Sir Walter, Elia, Wordsworth, Tennyson, Morris, and Jefferies. And, even in the colonies, they might demand to see "the code of taste resting on any solid foundation which proves" that you shall have any garden or park at all!

"If I am to have a system at all," says the author of "The Flower Garden" (Murray, 1852) whose broad-minded views declare him to be an amateur, "give me the good old system of terraces and angled walks, the clipt yew hedges, against whose dark and rich verdure the bright old-fashioned flowers glittered in the sun." Or again: "Of all the vain assumptions of these coxcomical times, that which arrogates the pre-eminence in the true science of gardening is the vainest. . . . The real beauty and poetry of a garden are lost in our efforts after rarity. If we review the various styles that have prevailed in England from the knotted gardens of Elizabeth . . . to the landscape fashion of the present day, we shall have little reason to pride ourselves on the advance which national taste has made upon the earliest efforts in this department" ("The Praise of Gardens," p. 270).

"Large or small," says Mr. W. Morris, "the garden should look both orderly and rich. It should be well fenced from the outer world. It should by no means imitate either the wilfulness or the wildness of Nature, but should look like a thing never seen except near a house" ("Hopes and Fears").

The whole point of the matter is, however, perhaps best summed up in Hazlitt's remark, that there is a pleasure in Art which none but artists feel. And why this sudden respect for "the materials of our world-designer," when we may ask in Repton's words "why this art has been called Landscape-gardening, perhaps he who gave the title may explain. I see no reason, unless it be the efficacy which it has shown in destroying landscapes, in which indeed it is infallible!" But, setting aside the transparent shallowness of such a plea against the use of Art in a garden, it argues little for the scheme of effects to leave "nothing to impede the view of the house or its windows but a refreshing carpet of grass." To pitch your house down upon the grass with no architectural accessories about it, to link it to the soil, is to vulgarise it, to rob it of importance, to give it the look of a pastoral farm, green to the door-step. To bring Nature up to the windows of your house, with a scorn of art-sweetness, is not only to betray your own deadness to form, but to cause a sense of unexpected blankness in the visitor's mind on leaving the well-appointed interior of an English home. As the house is an Art-production, so is the garden that surrounds it, and there is no code of taste that I know of which would prove that Art is more reprehensible in the garden than in the house.

But to return. The old-fashioned country house had its terraces. These terraces are not mere narrow slopes of turf, such as now-a-days too often answer to the term, but they are of solid masonry with balustrades or open-work that give an agreeable variety of light and shade, and impart an air of importance and of altitude to the house that would be lacking if the terrace were not there.

The whole of the ground upon which the house

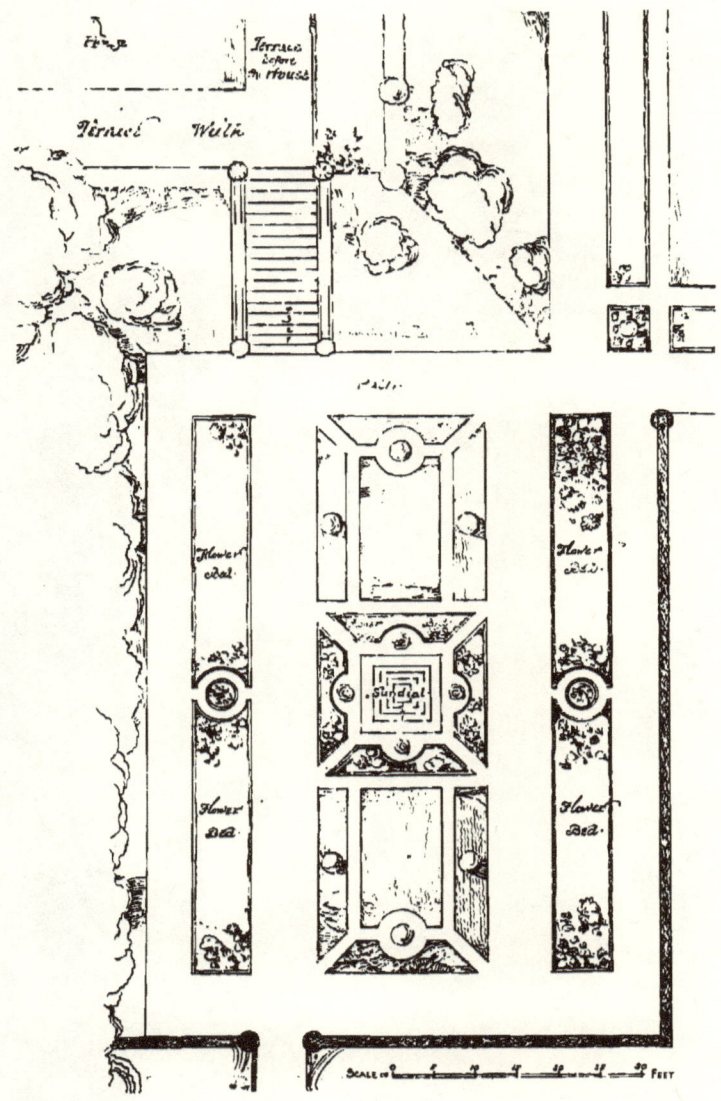

(Perspective view.)
No. 1. Plan of Rosery with Sundial.

Perspective view of Garden in Plan No. 1.

stands, or which forms its base, constitutes the terrace. In such cases the terrace-walls are usually in two or more levels, the upper terrace being mostly parallel with the line of the house, or bowed out at intervals with balconies, while the lower terrace, or terraces, serve as the varying levels of formal gardens, pleasure-grounds, labyrinths, &c. The terraces are approached by wide steps that are treated in a stately and impressive manner. The walls and balustrades, moreover, conform, as they should, to the materials employed in the house; if the house be of stone, as at Haddon, or Brympton, or Claverton, the balustrade is of stone; if the house be of brick, as at Hatfield or Bramshill, the walls and balustrades will be of brick and terra-cotta. The advantage of this agreement of material is obvious, for house and terrace, embraced at one glance, make a consistent whole. There is not, of course, the same necessity for consistency of material in the case of the mere retaining walls.

As one must needs have a system in planning grounds, there is none that will more certainly bring honour and effect to them than the regular geometrical treatment. This is what the architect naturally prefers. The house is his child, and he knows what is good for it. Unlike the imported gardener, who comes upon the scene as a foreign agent, the architect works from the house outwards, taking the house as his centre; the other works from the outside inwards, if he thinks of the "inwards" at all. The first thinks of house and grounds as a whole which shall embrace the main buildings, the out-buildings, the flower and kitchen-gardens, terraces, walls, forecourt, winter-garden, conservatory, fountain, steps, &c. The other makes the house common to the commonplace ; owing no allegiance to Art, a specialist of one idea, he holds that the worst thing that can be done is to intrude architectural or geometrical arrangement about a garden, and speaks of a refreshing carpet of grass as preferable.

As to the extent, number, and situation of terraces, this point is determined by the conditions of the house and site. Terraces come naturally if the house be on an eminence, but even in cases where the ground recedes only to a slight extent, the surface of a second terrace may be lowered by increasing the fall of the slope till sufficient earth is provided for the requisite filling. The surplus earth dug out in forming the foundations and cellars of the house, or rubbish from an old building, will help to make up the terrace levels and save the cost of wheeling and carting the rubbish away.

Like all embankments, terrace walls are built with "battered" fronts or outward slope ; the back of the wall will be left rough, and well drained. A backing of sods, Mr. Milner says, will prevent thrust, and admit of a lessened thickness in the wall. The walls should not be less than three feet in height from the ground-level beneath, exclusive of the balustrade, which is another three feet high.

The length of the terrace adds importance to the house, and in small gardens, where the kitchen-

No. 7. Plan of Tennis Lawn, Terraces, and Flower Garden.

garden occupies one side of the flower-garden, the terrace may with advantage be carried to the full extent of the ground, and the kitchen-garden separated by a hedge and shrubs; and at the upper end of the kitchen-garden may be a narrow garden, geometrical, rock, or other garden set next the terrace wall.

The treatment of the upper terrace should be strictly architectural. If the terrace be wide, raised beds with stone edging, set on the inner side of the terrace, say alternately long beds with dwarf flowering shrubs or hydrangeas, and circles with standard hollies, or marble statues on pedestals, that shall alternate with pyramidal golden yews, have a good effect, the terrace terminating with an arbour or stone Pavilion. Modern taste, however, even if it condescend so far as to allow of a terrace, is content with its grass plot and gravel walks, which is not carrying Art very far.

Laneham tells of the old pleasaunce at Kenilworth, that it had a terrace 10 ft. high and 12 ft. wide on the garden side, in which were set at intervals obelisks and spheres and white bears, "all of stone, upon their curious bases," and at each end an arbour; the garden-plot was below this, and had its fair alleys, or grass, or gravel.

The lower terrace may well be twice the width of the upper one, and may be a geometrical garden laid out on turf, if preferred, but far better upon gravel. Here will be collected the choicest flowers in the garden, giving a mass of rich colouring.

Although in old gardens the lower terrace is some 10 ft. below the upper one, this is too deep to suit modern taste; indeed, 5 ft. or 6 ft. will give a better view of the garden if it is to be viewed from the house. At the same time it is undeniable that the more you are able to look *down* upon the garden —the higher you stand above its plane—the better the effect; the lower you stand, the poorer the perspective.

Modern taste, also, will not always tolerate a balustraded wall as a boundary to the terrace, but likes a grass slope. If this poor substitute be preferred, there should be a level space at the bottom of the slope and at the top; the slope should have a continuous line, and not follow any irregularity in the natural lie of the ground, and there should be a simple plinth 12 to 18 in. high at the bottom of the slope.

But the mere grass slope does not much help the effect of the house, far or near; a house standing on a grass slope always has the effect of sliding down a hill. To leave the house exposed upon the landscape, unscreened and unterraced, is not to treat site or house fairly. There exists a certain necessity for features in a flat place, and if no raised terrace be possible, it is desirable to get architectural treatment by means of balustrades alone, without much, or any, fall in the ground. The eye always asks for definite boundaries to a piece of ornamental ground as it does for a frame to a picture, and where definite boundaries do not exist, the distant effect is that of a

No. 5. General Plan of the Great Hall of the Villa Borghese and its surrounding Gardens.

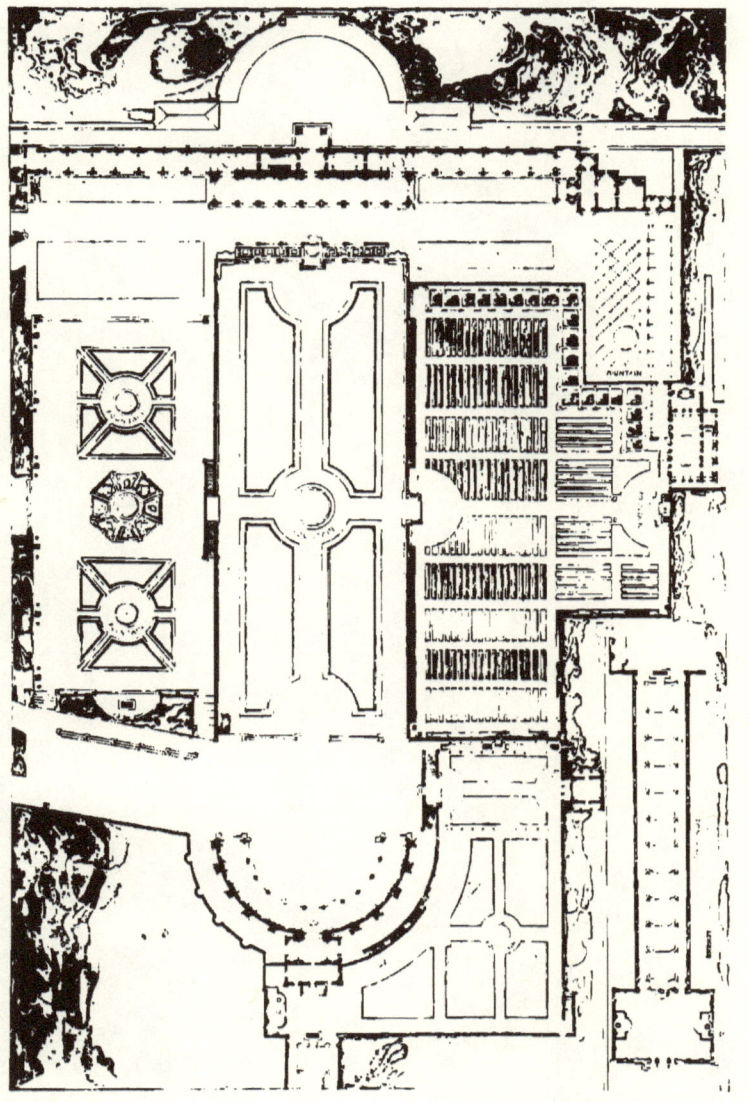

No. 3. General Plan of the Pleasaunce, Villa Albani, Rome.

house that has tumbled casually down from the skies, near which the cattle may graze as they list, and the flower-beds are the mere sport of contingencies.

Good examples of terrace walls are to be found at Haddon, Claverton, Brympton, Montacute, Bramshill, Wilton, and Blickling Hall. If truth be told, however, all our English examples dwindle into nothingness by the side of fine Italian examples like those at Villa Albani,* Villa Medici, or Villa Borghese, with their grand scope and array of sculpture. (See illustration from Percier and Fontaine's " *Choix des plus célèbres maisons de plaisance de Rome et de ses environs.*" Paris, MDCCCIX.)

The arrangements of steps is a matter that may call forth a man's utmost ingenuity. The scope and variety of step arrangement is, indeed, a matter that can only be realised by designers who have given it their study. As to practical points. In planning steps make the treads wide, the risers low. Long flights without landings are always objectionable. Some of the best examples, both in England and abroad, have winders; as to the library quadrangle, Trinity Coll., Cambridge; Donibristle Castle, Scotland; Villa d'Este, Tivoli; the gardens at Nîmes. The grandest specimen of all is the Trinità di Monte steps in Rome (see Notes on Gardens in *The British Architect*, by John Belcher and Mervyn Macartney).

It is impossible to lay down rules of equal application everywhere as to the distribution of garden

---

* See accompanying plans.

M

area into compartments, borders, terraces, walks, &c. These matters are partly regulated by the character of the house, its situation, the section and outline of the ground. But gardens should, if possible, lie towards the best parts of the house, or towards the rooms most commonly in use by the family, and endeavour should be made to plant them so that to step from the house on to the terrace, or from the terrace to the various parts of the gardens, should only seem like going from one room to another.

Of the arrangement of the ground into divisions, each section should have its own special attractiveness and should be led up to by some inviting artifice of archway, or screened alley of shrubs, or "rosery" with its trellis-work, or stone colonnade; and if the alley be long it should be high enough to afford shade from the glare of the sun in hot weather; you ought not, as Bacon pertinently says, to "buy the shade by going into the sun."

Again, the useful and the beautiful should be happily united, the kitchen and the flower garden, the way to the stables and outbuildings, the orchard, the winter garden, &c., all having a share of consideration and a sense of connectedness; and if there be a chance for a filbert walk, seize it; that at Hatfield is charming. "I cannot understand," says Richard Jefferies ("Wild Life in a Southern County," p. 70), "why filbert walks are not planted by our modern capitalists, who make nothing of spending a thousand pounds in forcing-houses."

A garden should be well fenced, and there should

always be facility for getting real seclusion, so much needed now-a-days; indeed, the provision of places of retreat has always been a note of an English garden. The love of retirement, almost as much as a taste for trees and flowers, has dictated its shapes. Hence the *cedar-walks, the bower, the avenue, the maze, the alley, the wilderness, that were familiar, and almost the invariable features of an old English pleasaunce, " hidden happily and shielded safe."

This seclusion can be got by judicious screening of parts, by shrubberies, or avenues of hazel, or yew, or sweet-scented bay, with perhaps clusters of lilies and hollyhocks, or dwarf Alpine plants and trailers between. And in all this the true gardener will have a thought for the birds. " No modern exotic evergreens," says Jefferies, " ever attract our English birds like the true old English trees and shrubs. In the box and yew they love to build; spindly laurels and rhododendrons, with vacant draughty spaces underneath, they detest, avoiding them as much as possible. The common hawthorn hedge round a country garden shall contain three times as many nests, and be visited by five times as many birds as the foreign evergreens, so costly to rear and so sure to be killed by the first old-fashioned frost."

* One of the finest and weirdest cedar-walks that I have ever met with is that at Marwell, near Owslebury in Hampshire. Here you realize the wizardry of green gloom and sense of perfect seclusion. It was here that Henry VIII. courted one of his too willing wives.

Another chance for getting seclusion is the high walls or lofty yew hedge of the quadrangular courtyard, which may be near the entrance. Such a forecourt is the place for a walk on bleak days; in its borders you are sure of the earliest spring flowers, for the tender flowers can here bloom securely, the myrtle, the pomegranate will flourish, and the most fragrant plants and climbers hang over the door and windows. What is more charming than the effect of hollyhocks, peonies, poppies, tritomas, and tulips seen against a yew hedge?

The paths should be wide and excellently made. The English have always had good paths; as Mr. Evelyn said to Mr. Pepys, "We have the best walks of gravell in the world, France having none, nor Italy." The comfort and the elegance of a garden depend in no slight degree upon good gravel walks, but having secured gravel walks to all parts of the grounds, green alleys should also be provided. Nothing is prettier than a vista through the smooth-shaven green alley, with a statue or sundial or pavilion at the end; or an archway framing a peep of the country beyond.

As to the garden's size, it is erroneous to suppose that the enjoyments of a garden are only in proportion to its magnitude; the pleasurableness of a garden depends infinitely more upon the degree of its culture and the loving care that is bestowed upon it. If gardens were smaller than they usually are, there would be a better chance of their orderly keeping. As it is, gardens are mostly too large for

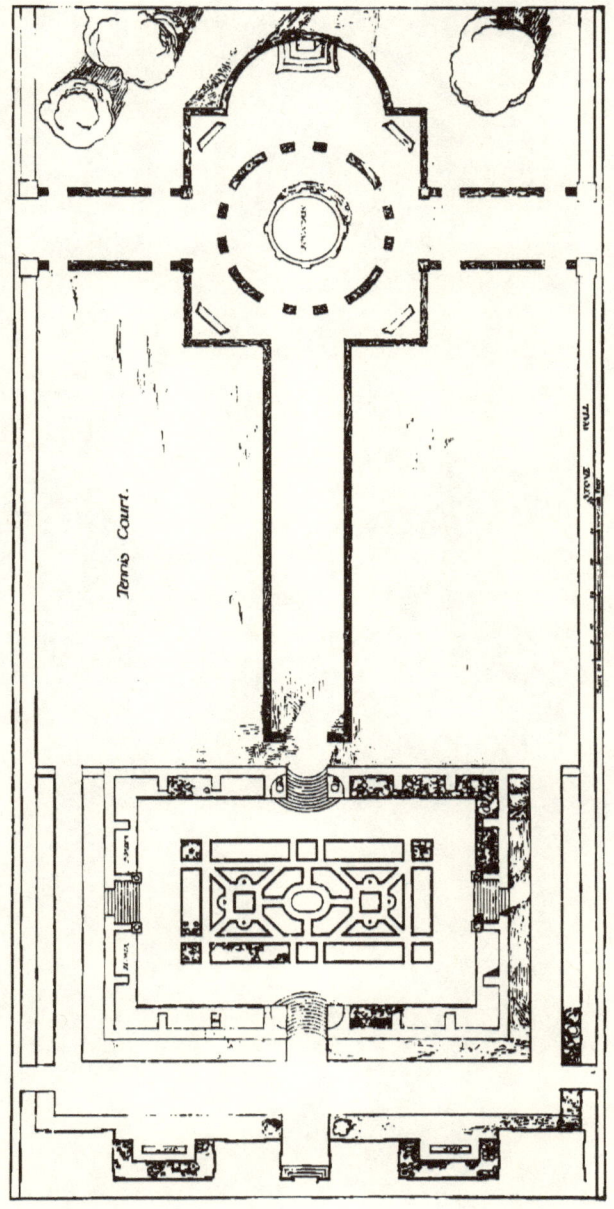

No. 4. Plan shewing arrangement of Sunk Flower Garden, Yew Walk, and Tennis Court.

the number of attendants, so that the time and care of the gardener are nearly absorbed in the manual labour of repairing and stocking the beds, and maintaining and sweeping the walks.

But if not large, the grounds should not have the appearance of being confined within a limited space; and Art is well spent in giving an effect of greater extent to the place than it really possesses by a suitable composition of the walks, bushes, and trees. These lines should lead the eye to the distance, and if bounded by trees, the garden should be connected with the outer world by judicious openings; and this rule applies to gardens large or small.

Ground possessing a gentle inclination towards the south is desirable for a garden. On such a slope effectual drainage is easily accomplished, and the greatest possible benefit obtained from the sun's rays. The garden should, if possible, have an open exposure towards the east and west, so that it may enjoy the full benefit of morning and evening sun; but shelter on the north or north-east, or any side in which the particular locality may happen to be exposed, is desirable.

The dimensions of the garden will be proportionate to the scale of the house. The general size of the garden to a good-sized house is from four to six acres, but the extent varies in many places from twelve to twenty, or even thirty acres. (See an admirable article on gardening in the "Encyclopædia."

Before commencing to lay out a garden the plan should be prepared in minute detail, and every point carefully considered. Two or three acres of kitchen garden, enclosed by walls and surrounded by slips, will suffice for the supply of a moderate establishment.* The form of the kitchen garden advocated by the writer in the "Encyclopædia" is that of a square, or oblong, not curvilinear, since the work of cropping of the ground can thus be more easily carried out. On the whole, the best form is that of a parallelogram, with its longest sides in the proportion of about five to three of the shorter, and running east and west. The whole should be compactly arranged so as to facilitate working, and to afford convenient access for the carting of heavy materials to the store-yards, etc.

There can, as we have said, be no fixed or uniform arrangement of gardens. Some grounds will have more flower-beds than others, some more park or wilderness; some will have terraces, some not; some a pinetum, or an American garden. In some gardens the terraces will lie immediately below the main front of the house, in others not, because the geometrical garden needs a more sheltered site where the flowers can thrive.

---

* As the walls afford valuable space for the growth of the choicer kinds of hardy fruits, the direction in which they are built is of considerable importance. "In the warmer parts of the country, the wall on the north side of the garden should be so placed as to face the sun at about an hour before noon, or a little to east of south; in less favoured localities it should be made to face direct south, and in the still more unfavourable districts it should face the sun an hour after noon, or a little west of south. The east and west walls should run parallel to each other, and at right angles to that on the north side."

(Perspective view.)
No. 2. Plan of Sunk Flower Garden and Yew Hedges.

Perspective view of Sunk Garden in Plan No. 2.

Of the shapes of the beds it were of little avail to speak, and the diagrams here given are only of use where the conditions of the ground properly admit of their application. The geometrical garden is capable of great variety of handling. A fair size for a geometrical garden is 120 ft. by 60 ft. This size will allow of a main central walk of seven feet that shall divide the panel into two equal parts and lead down to the next level. The space may have a balustrade along its length on the two sides, and on the garden side of the balustrade a flower-bed of mixed flowers and choice low-growing shrubs, backed with hollyhocks, tritoma, lilies, golden-rod, etc. The width of the border will correspond with the space required for the steps that descend from the upper terrace. For obtaining pleasant proportions in the design, the walks in the garden will be of two sizes, gravelled like the rest—the wider walk, say, three feet, the smaller one foot nine inches. The centre of the garden device on each side may be a raised bed with a stone kerb and an ornamental shrub in the middle, and the space around with, say, periwinkle or stonecrop, mixed with white harebells, or low creepers. Or, should there be no wide main walk, and the garden-plot be treated as one composition, the central bed will have a statue, sundial, fountain, or other architectural feature. Each bed will be edged with box or chamfered stone, or terra-cotta edging. Or the formal garden may be sunk below the level of the paths, and filled either with flowers or with dwarf coniferæ.

Both for practical and artistic reasons, the beds should not be too small; they should not be so small that, when filled with plants, they should appear like spots of colour, nor be so large that any part of them cannot be easily reached by a rake. Nor should the shapes of the beds be too angular to accommodate the plants well. In Sir Gardner Wilkinson's book on "Colour" (Murray, 1858, p. 372), he speaks of design and good form as the very *soul* of a dressed garden; and the very permanence of the forms, which remain though successive series of plants be removed, calls for a good design. The shapes of the beds, as well as the colours of their contents, are taken cognisance of in estimating the general effect of a geometrical garden. This same accomplished author advises that there should always be a less formal garden beyond the geometrical one; the latter is, so to speak, an appurtenance of the house, a feature of the plateau upon which it stands, and no attempt should be made to combine the patterns of the geometrical with the beds or borders of the outer informal garden, such combination being specially ill-judged in the neighbourhood of bushes and winding paths.

Of the proper selection of flowers and the determination of the colours for harmonious combination in the geometrical beds, much that is contradictory has been preached, one gardener leaning to more formality than another. There is, however, a general agreement upon the necessity of having beds that will look fairly well at all seasons of the year, and an agreement as to the use of hardy flowers in these beds. Mr. Robinson has some good advice to give upon this point ("English Flower Garden," p. 24) : "The ugliest and most needless parterre (!) in England may be planted in the most beautiful way with hardy flowers alone." (Why "needless," then ?) "Are we not all wrong in adopting one degree, so to say, of plant life as the only fitting one to lay before the house ? Is it well to devote the flower-bed to one type of vegetation only—low herbaceous vegetation—be that hardy or tender ? . . . We have been so long accustomed to leave flower-beds raw, and to put a number of plants out every year, forming flat surfaces of colour, that no one even thinks of the higher and better way of filling them. But surely it is worth considering whether it would not be right to fill the beds permanently, rather than to leave them in this naked or flat condition throughout the whole of the year. . . . If any place asks for permanent planting, it is the spot of ground immediately near the house ; for no one can wish to see large, grave-like masses of soil frequently dug and disturbed near the windows, and few care for the result of all this, even when the ground is well covered during a good season." Again our author, on p. 95, states that "he has very decided notions as to arrangement of the various colours for summer bedding, which are that the whole shall be so commingled that one would be puzzled to determine what tint predominates in the entire arrangement." He would have a "glaucous" colour, that is, a light grey or whitish green. Such a colour never tires the eye, and harmonises with the tints of the landscape, "particularly of the lawn." This seems to be neutralising the effects of the flowers, and this primal consideration of the lawn is like scorning your picture for the sake of its frame!

Sir Gardner Wilkinson, who writes of gardens from quite another point of view, says: "It is by no means necessary or advisable to select rare flowers for the beds, and some of the most common are the most eligible, being more hardy, and therefore less likely to fail, or to cover the bed with a scanty and imperfect display of colour. Indeed, it is a common mistake to seek rare flowers, when many of the old and most ordinary varieties are far more beautiful. The point to note in this matter of choosing flowers for a geometrical garden is to ascertain first the lines that will best accord with the design, and make for a harmonious and brilliant effect, and to see that the flowers best suited to it blossom at the same periods. A succession of those of the same colour may be made to take the place of each, and continue the design at successive seasons. They should also be, as near as possible, of the same height as their companions, so that the blue flowers be not over tall in one bed, or the red too short in another. . . . Common flowers, the weeds of the country, are often most beautiful in colour, and are not to be despised because they are common; they have also the advantage of being hardy, and rare flowers are not always those

Perspective view of part of Garden at " Downes," Hayle.

best suited for beds" (Wilkinson on "Colour," p. 375).

With regard to the ornamental turf-beds of our modern gardens. To judge of a garden upon high principles, we expect it to be the finest and fittest expression that a given plot of ground will take; it must be the perfect adaptation of means to an end, and that end is beauty. Are we to suppose, then, that the turf-beds of strange device that we meet with in modern gardens are the best that can be done by the heir of all the ages in the way of garden-craft? A garden, I am aware, has other things to attend to besides the demands of ideal beauty; it has to embellish life to supply innocent pleasure to the inmates of the house as well as to dignify the house itself; and the devising of these vagrant beds that sprawl about the grounds is a pleasure that can be ill spared from the artistic delights of a modern householder. It is indeed wonderful to what heights the British fancy can rise when put to the push, if only it have a congenial field! So here we have flower-beds shaped as crescents and kidneys—beds like flying bats or bubbling tadpoles, commingled butterflies and leeches, stars and sausages, hearts and commas, monograms and maggots—a motley assortment to be sure—but the modern mind is motley, and the pretty flowers smile a sickly smile out of their comic beds, as though Paradise itself could provide them with no fairer lodgings!

And yet if I dare speak my mind "sike fancies weren foolerie;" and it were hard to find a good word to say for them from any point of view whatever. Their wobbly shapes are not elegant; they have not the sanction of precedent, even of epochs the most barbarous. And though they make pretence at being a species of art, their mock-formality has not that geometric precision which shall bind them to the formal lines of the house, or to the general bearings of the site. Not only do they contribute nothing to the artistic effect of the general design, but they even mar the appearance of the grass that accommodates them. Design they have, but not design of that quality which alone justifies its intrusion. No wonder "Nature abhors lines" if this base and spurious imitation of the "old formality," that Charles Lamb gloats over, is all that the landscape-garden can offer in the way of idealisation.

One other feature of the old-fashioned garden—the herbaceous border—requires a word. It is worthy of note that, unlike the modern, the ancient gardener was not a man of one idea—his art is not bounded like a barrel-organ that can only play one invariable tune! While the master of the "old formality" can give intricate harmonies of inwoven colours in the geometric beds—"all mosaic, choicely planned," where Nature lends her utmost magic to grace man's fancy—he knows the value of the less as well as the more, and finds equal room for the unconstrained melodies of odd free growths in the border-beds, where you shall enjoy the individual character, the form, the outline, the colour, the tone of each plant. Here let the mind of an earlier generation speak in George Milner's "Country Pleasures":

"By this time I have got round to the old English flower-bed, where only perennials with an ancient ancestry are allowed to grow. Here there is always delight; and I should be sorry to exchange its sweet flowers for any number of cartloads of scentless bedding-plants, mechanically arranged and ribbon-bordered. This bed is from fifty to sixty yards long, and three or four yards in width. A thorn hedge divides it from the orchard. In spring the apple-bloom hangs over, and now we see in the background the apples themselves. The plants still in flower are the dark blue monkshood, which is 7ft. high; the spiked veronica; the meadow-sweet or queen-o'-the-meadow; the lady's mantle, and the evening primrose. This last may be regarded as the characteristic plant of the season. The flowers open about seven o'clock, and as the twilight deepens, they gleam like pale lamps, and harmonise wonderfully with the colour of the sky. *On this bed I read the history of the year.* Here were the first snowdrops; here came the crocuses, the daffodils, the blue gentians, the columbines, the great globed peonies; and last, the lilies and the roses."

And now to apply what has been said.

Since gardening entails so much study and experience—since it is a craft in which one is so apt to err, in small matters as in large—since it exists to represent passages of Nature that have touched man's imagination from time immemorial—since its business is to paint living pictures of living things whose habits, aspects, qualities, and character have ever engaged man's interest—since the modern gardener has not only not found new sources of inspiration unknown of old, but has even lost sensibility to some that were active then—it were surely wise to take the hand of old garden-masters who did large things in a larger past—to whom fine gardening came as second nature—whose success has given English garden-craft repute which not even the journeyman efforts of modern times can quite extinguish.

These men—Bacon, Temple, Evelyn, and their school—let us follow for style, elevated form, noble ideals, and artistic interpretation of Nature.

For practical knowledge of trees and shrubs, indigenous or exotic—to know *how* to plant and *what* to plant—to know what to avoid in the practice of modern blunderers—to know the true theory and practice of Landscape-gardening, reduced to writing, after ample analysis—turn we to those books of solid value of the three great luminaries of modern garden-craft, Gilpin, Repton, Loudon.

And it were not only to be ungenerous, but absolutely foolish, to neglect the study of the best that is now written and done in the way of landscape-gardening, in methods of planting, and illustration of botany up to date. One school may see things from a different point of view to another, yet is there but one art of gardening. It is certain that to gain boldness in practice, to have clear views upon that delicate point—the relations of Art and Nature—to have a reliable standard of excellence, we must know and value the good in the garden-craft of all times, must sympathise with the point of view of each phase, and follow that which is good in each and all without scruple and doubtfulness. That man is a fool who thinks that he can escape the influence of his day, or that he can dispense with tradition.

I say, let us follow the old garden-masters for

style, form, ideal, and artistic interpretation of Nature, and let us not say what Horace Walpole whimpered forth of Temple's garden-enterprise: "These are adventures of too hard achievement for any common hands." Have we not seen that at the close of Bacon's lessons in grand gardening he adds, that the things thrown in "for state and magnificence" are but nothing to the true pleasure of a garden?

The counsels of perfection are not to be slighted because our ground is small. In gardening, as in other matters, the true test of one's work is the measure of one's possibilities. A small, trim garden, like a sonnet, may contain the very soul of beauty. A small garden may be as truly admirable as a perfect song or painting.

Let it be our aim, then, to give to gardening all the method and distinctness of which it is capable, and admit no impediments. A garden not fifty yards square, deftly handled, judiciously laid out, its beds and walks suitably directed, will yield thrice the opportunity for craft, thrice the scope for imaginative endeavour that a two-acre "garden" of the pastoral-farm order, such as is recommended of the faculty, will yield. The very division of the ground into proportionate parts, the varied levels obtained, the framed vistas, the fitting architectural adjuncts, will alone contribute an air of size and scale. As to "codes of taste" (which are usually in matters of Art only someone's opinions stated pompously), these should not be allowed to baulk individual enterprise. "Long experience," says that accomplished gardener and charming writer, E. V. B., in "Days and Hours in a Garden" (p. 125), "Long experience has taught me to have nothing to do with principles in the garden. Little else than a feeling of entire sympathy with the diverse characters of your plants and flowers is needed for 'Art in a Garden.' If sympathy be there, all the rest comes naturally enough." Or to put this thought in Temple's words, "The success is wholly in the gardener."

If a garden grow flowers in abundance, *there* is success, and one may proceed to frame a garden after approved "codes of taste" and fail in this, or one may prefer unaccepted methods and find success beyond one's fondest dreams. "All is fine that is fit" is a good garden motto; and what an eclectic principle is this! How many kinds of style it allows, justifies, and guards! the simplest way or the most ornate; the fanciful or the sweet austere; the intricate and complex, or the coy and unconstrained. Take it as true as Gospel that there is danger in the use of ornament—danger of excess—take it as equally true that there is an intrinsic and superior value in moderation, and yet the born gardener shall find more paths, old and new, that lead to Beauty in a plot of garden-ground than the modern stylist dreams of.

The art of gardening may now be known of all men. Gardening is no longer a merely princely diversion requiring thirty wide acres for its display. Everyone who can, now lives in the country, where he is bound to have a garden; and I repeat what I said before, let no one suppose that the beauty of a garden depends on its acreage, or on the amount of money spent upon it. Nay, one would almost prefer a small garden plot, so as to ensure that ample justice shall be done to it.* In a small garden there is less fear of dissipated effort, more chance of making friends with its inmates, more time to spare to heighten the beauty of its effects.

To some extent the success of a garden depends upon favourable conditions of sun, soil, and water, but more upon the choiceness of its contents, the skill of its planting, the lovingness of its tendence. Love for beauty has a way of enticing beauty; the seeing eye wins its own ranges of vision, finds points of vantage in unlikely ground. "I write in a nook," says the poet Cowper, "that I call my boudoir; it is a summer-house, not bigger than a sedan-chair; the door of it opens into the garden that is now crowded with pinks, roses, and honeysuckles, *and the window into my neighbour's orchard.* It formerly served an apothecary as a smoking-room; at present, however, it is dedicated to sublimer uses." What a mastery of life is here!

> "As if life's business were a summer mood;
> As if all needful things would come unsought
> To genial faith, still rich in genial good;
> . . . . . .
> By our own spirits are we deified."

But I must not finish the stanza in this connection.

* "Embower a cottage thickly and completely with nothing but roses, and nobody would desire the interference of another plant."
—LEIGH HUNT.

A garden is pre-eminently a place to indulge individual taste. "Let us not be that fictitious thing," says Madame Roland, "that can only exist by the help of others—*soyons nous!*" So, regardless of the doctors, let me say that the best general rule that I can devise for garden-making is: put all the beauty and delightsomeness you can into your garden, get all the beauty and delight you can out of your garden, never minding a little mad want of balance, and think of proprieties afterwards! Of course, this is to "prove naething," but never mind if but the garden enshrine beauty. To say this is by no means to allow that the garden is the fit place for indulging your love of the out-of-the-way; not so, yet a little sign of fresh motive, a touch of individual technique, a token, however shyly displayed, that you think for yourself is welcome in a garden. Thus I know of a gardener who turned a section of his grounds into a sort of huge bear-pit, not a sunk pit, but a mound that took the refuse soil from the site of his new house hollowed out, and its slopes set all round with Alpine and American garden-plants, each variety finding the aspect it likes best, and the proportion of light and shade that suits its constitution. This is, of course, to "intrude embankments" into a garden with a vengeance, yet even Mr. Robinson, if he saw it, would allow that, as in love and war, your daring in gardening is justified by its results, where, as George Herbert has it—

> "Who shuts his hand, hath lost its gold;
> Who opens it, hath it twice told."

A garden is, first and last, a place for flowers; but, treading in the old master's footsteps, I would devote a certain part of even a small garden to Nature's own wild self, and the loveliness of weed-life. Here Art should only give things a good start and help the propagation of some sorts of plants not indigenous to the locality. Good effects do not ensue all at once, but stand aside and wait, or help judiciously, and the result will be a picture of rude and vigorous life, of pretty colour and glorious form, that is gratifying for its own qualities, and more for its opposition to the peacefulness of the garden's ordered surroundings.

A garden is the place for flowers, a place where one may foster a passion for loveliness, may learn the magic of colour and the glory of form, and quicken sympathy with Nature in her higher moods. And, because the old-fashioned garden more conduces to these ends than the modern, it has our preference. The spirit of old garden-craft says: "Do everything that can be done to help Nature, to lift things to perfection, to interpret, to give to your Art method and distinctness." The spirit of the modern garden-craft of the purely landscape school says: "Let be, let well alone, or extemporise at most. Brag of your scorn for Art, yet smuggle her in, as a stalking-horse for your halting method and non-geometrical forms."

And, as we have shown, Art has her revenges as well as Nature; and the very negativeness of this school's Art-treatments is the seal to its doom.

Mere neutral teaching can father nothing; it can never breed a system of stable device that is capable of development. But old garden-craft is positive, where the other is negative; it has no niggling scruples, but clear aims, that admit of no impediment except the unwritten laws of good taste. Hence its permanent value as a standard of device—for every gardener must needs desire the support of some backbone of experience to stiffen his personal efforts—he must needs have some basis of form on which to rest his own device, his own realisations of natural beauty—and what safer, stabler system of garden-craft can he wish for than that of the old English garden—itself the outcome of a spacious age, well skilled in the pictorial art and bent upon perfection?

The qualities to aim at in a flower-garden are beauty, animation, variety, mystery. A garden's beauty, like a woman's beauty, is measured by its capacity for taking fine dress. Given a fine garden, and we need not fear to use embellishment or strong colour, or striking device, according to the adage "The richly provided richly require."

Because Art stands, so to speak, sponsor for the grace of a garden, because all gardening is Art or nothing, we need not fear to overdo Art in a garden, nor need we fear to make avowal of the secret of its charm. I have no more scruple in using the scissors upon tree or shrub, where trimness is desirable, than I have in mowing the turf of the lawn that once represented a virgin world. There is a quaint charm in the results of the topiary art, in the prim imagery

Perspective view of Garden in Plan No. 6.

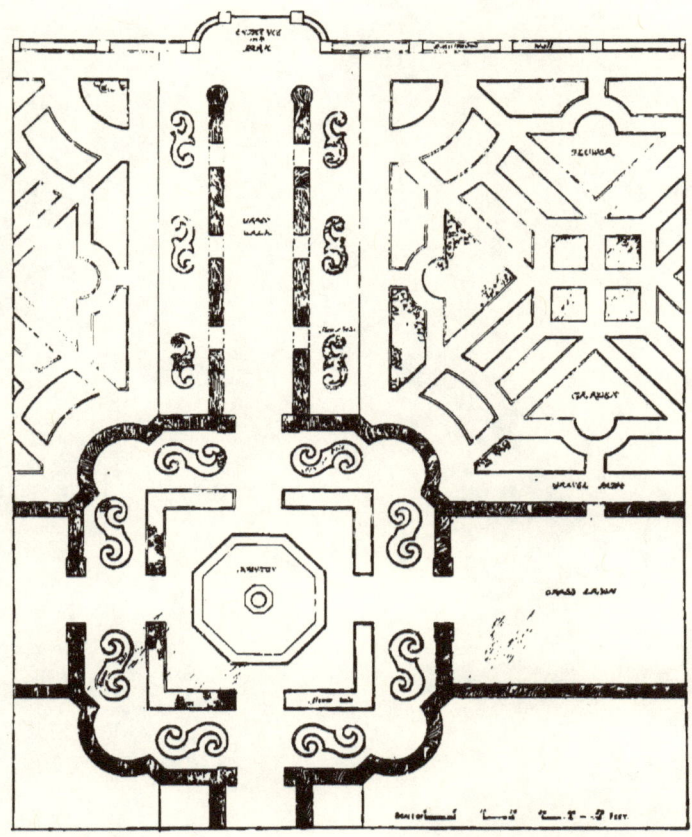

(Perspective view.)
No. 6. Plan shewing arrangement of Fountain, Yew Walk, and Flower Beds for a Large Garden.

of evergreens, that all ages have felt. And I would even introduce *bizarreries* on the principle of not leaving all that is wild and odd to Nature outside of the garden-paling; and in the formal part of the garden my yews should take the shape of pyramids or peacocks or cocked hats or ramping lions in Lincoln-green, or any other conceit I had a mind to, which vegetable sculpture can take.

As to the other desirable qualities—animation, variety, mystery—I would base my garden upon the model of the old masters, without adopting any special style. The place should be a home of fancy, full of intention, full of pains (without showing any); half common-sense, half romance; "neither praise nor poetry, but something better than either," as Burke said of Sheridan's speech; it should have an ethereal touch, yet be not inappropriate for the joyous racket and country cordiality of an English home. It should be

"A miniature of loveliness, all grace
Summ'd up and closed in little"—

something that would challenge the admiration and suit the moods of various minds; be brimful of colour-gladness, yet be not all pyramids of sweets, but offer some solids for the solid man; combining old processes and new, old idealisms and new realisms; the monumental style of the old here, the happy-go-lucky shamblings of the modern there; the page of Bacon or Temple here, the page of Repton or Marnock there. At every turn the imagination should get a fresh stimulus to surprise; we should be led on from one fair sight, one attractive picture, to another; not suddenly, nor without some preparation of heightened expectancy, but as in a fantasy, and with something of the quick alternations of a dream.

Your garden, gentle reader, is perchance not yet made. It were indeed happiness if, when good things betide you, and the time is ripe for your enterprise, Art

. . . . "Shall say to thee
I find you worthy, do this thing for me."

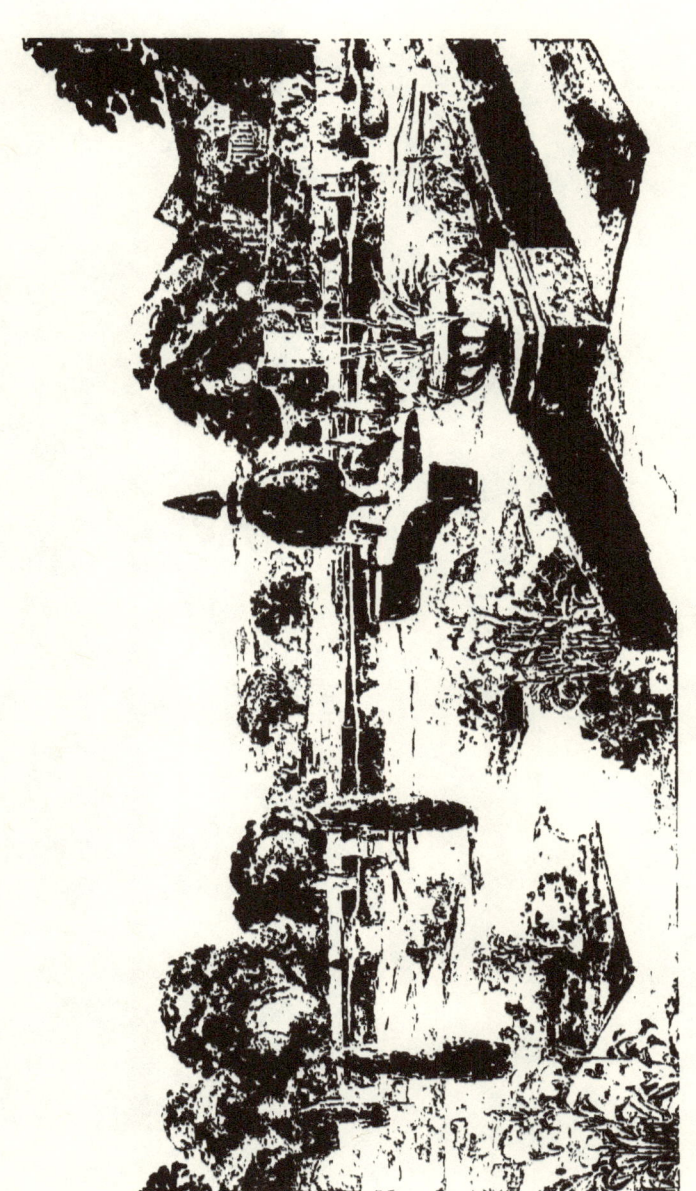

Perspective view of a Design for a Garden, with Clipped Yew Hedges and Flower Beds.

CHAPTER VIII.

ON THE OTHER SIDE.—A PLEA FOR SAVAGERY.

"I am tired of civilised Europe, and I want to see a wild country if I can."—W. R. GREG.

"Howsoever these things be, a long farewell to Locksley Hall!"—TENNYSON.

WE have discussed the theory of a garden; we have analysed the motives which prompt its making, the various treatments of which it is susceptible; we have made a kind of inventory of its effects, its enchantments, its spendthrift joys. Now we will hear the other side, and find out why the morbid, tired man, the modern Hamlet, likes it not, why the son of culture loathes it as a lack-lustre thing, betokening to him the sedentary and respectable world in its most hostile form. Having made our picture now we will turn it round, and note why it is that the garden, with its full complement of approved ornament, its selected vegetation, its pretty turns for Nature, its many-sided beauty—

> "Or gay, or grave, or sweet, or stern was there
> Not less than truth designed"

—shall never wholly satisfy.

Your garden will serve you in many ways. It will give a sense of household warmth to your home.

It will smile, or look grave, or be dreamily fanciful almost at your bidding. If your bent be that way it will minister to your imaginative reverie, and almost surfeit you with its floods of lazy music. If you are hot, or weary, or dispirited, or touched with *ennui*, its calm atmosphere will lay the dust, and lessen the fret of your life. Yet—let us not blink the fact— just because *all* Nature is not represented here; because the girdle of the garden walls narrows our view of the world at large, and excludes more of Nature's physiognomy than it includes; because the garden is, as Sir Walter truly says, entirely "a child of Art"; the place, be it never so fair, falls short of man's imaginative craving, and, when put to the push, fails to supply the stimulus his varying moods require. <u>Art's sounding-line will never fathom human nature's emotional depths.</u>

Nay, one need not be that interesting product of civilisation, the over-civilised artist who writes books, and paints pictures, and murmurs rhyme that—

> "Beats with light wing against the ivory gate,
> Telling a tale not too importunate
> To those who in the sleepy region stay,
> Lulled by the singer of an empty day."

There is the *ennuyé* of the clubs whom you are proud to meet in Pall Mall, not a hair of his hat turned, not a wrinkle marring the sit of his coat; meeting him thus and there you would not dream of supposing that this exquisite trophy of the times is a prey to reactionary desires! Yet deep down in the hidden roots of his being lies a layer of unscotched savagery—an unextinguished, inextinguishable strain of the wild man of the woods. Scratch him, and beneath his skin is Rousseau-Thoreau. Scratch him again in the same place, and beneath his second skin see the brown hide of the aboriginal Briton, the dweller in wattled abodes, who knew an earlier England than this, that had swamps and forests, roadless wastes and unbridled winter floods, and strange beasts that no man could tame. Even he ("the sweetest lamb that ever loved a bear") will prate to you of the Bohemian delights of an ungardened country, where "the white man's poetry" has not defiled the landscape, and the Britisher shall be free to take his pleasure sadly.

Let us not be too hard, then, on that dislike of beauty, that worship of the barbaric which we are apt to condemn as distempered vagaries, for they denote maladies incident to the age, which are neither surprising nor ignoble. This disdain for Art in a garden, this abhorrence of symmetry, this preference for the rude and shaggy, what is it but a new turn given to old instincts, the new Don Quixote sighing for primævalism! This ruthlessness of the followers of the "immortal Brown" who would navvy away the residue of the old-fashioned English gardens; who live to reverse tradition and to scatter the lessons of the past to the winds; what is it but a new quest of the bygone, the knight-errantry of the civilised man, when turned inside out!

And for yet another reason is the garden unable to meet the moods of the age. In discussing the things it may rightly contain, we saw that the laws of artistic presentment, no less than the avowed purpose for which a garden is made, require that only such things shall be admitted, or such aspects be portrayed there, as conduce to gladness and poetic charm. And, so far as the garden is concerned, the restriction is necessary and desirable. As with other phases of Art, Sculpture, Painting, or Romance, <u>the things and aspects portrayed</u> <u>must be idealistic, not realistic</u>; its effects must be select, not indiscriminate. The garden is a deliberately contrived thing, a voluntary piece of handicraft, purpose-made; and for this reason <u>it must not stereotype imperfections;</u> it may toy with Nature, but must not wilfully exaggerate what is ordinary; only Nature may exaggerate herself—not Art. <u>It must not imitate those items in Nature that are crude</u>, <u>ugly</u>, <u>abnormal</u>, <u>elementary</u>; it may not reproduce the absolutely repellent; or at most, the artist may only touch them with a light hand, by way of imaginative hint, but not with intent to produce a finished picture out of them.

On this point there is a distinct analogy between the guiding principles of Art and Religion. Art and Religion both signify effort to comply with an ideal standard—indeed, the height of the standard is the test of each—and what makes for innocence or for faultiness in the one, makes for innocence or faultiness in the other. Innocence is found in each, but to be without guile in Art or in Religion means that you must be either flawlessly obedient to a perfect standard, or be beyond the pale of law through pure ignorance of wrong. Where no law is, there can be no transgression. Between these two points is no middle-ground, either in the fields of Art or of Religion.

To apply this to a garden. Untaught, lawless Nature may present things indiscriminately, as they are, the casual, the accidental, the savage, in their native dress, or undress, in all their rugged reality, and not be ashamed. But the artist-gardener, knowing good and evil, exercising free-will in his garden-craft, must choose only what he may rightly have, and employ only what his trained judgment or the unwritten commandments of good taste will allow.

There you have the art of a garden. But because of its necessary exclusiveness, because all Nature is not there, the garden, though of the best, the most far-reaching in its application of art-resources, fails to satisfy all man's imaginative cravings.

Your garden, I said, will serve you many a good turn. Here one may come to play the truant from petty worries, to find quiet harbourage in the chopping sea of life's casual ups and downs; but when *real* trouble comes, on occasions of spiritual tension, or mental conflict, or heavy depression, then the perfect beauty of the garden offends; the garden has no respect for sadness—then it almost mocks and flaunts you; it smiles the same, though your child die, and then instinct sends you away from the lap of Art to the bosom of Nature—

> "Knowing that Nature never did betray
> The heart that loved her."

All of man, then, asks for all of Nature, and is not content with less. Just as a stringed instrument, even when lying idle, is awake to sympathetic sound but refuses to vibrate to notes that are not kindred to its compass, so the garden, with all its wakeful magic, will voice only such of your moods as it is in touch with; and there are many chords missing in the cunningly encased music of a garden—many human notes find no answering pulsation there.

Let us not blink the fact, then; Art, whether of this sphere or of that, is not all. If you want beauty ready-made, obvious gladness of colour, heightened nobleness of form, suggested romance, Nature idealised—all these things are yours in a garden; and yet the very "dressing" of the place which heightens its appeal to one side of man's being is the bar to its acceptance on another side. To have been baptised of Art is to have received gifts rich and strange, that enable the garden's contents to climb to ideal heights; and yet not all men care for perfectness; the most part prefer creatures not too bright or good for human nature's daily food. So, to tell truth, the wild things of field, forest, and shore have a gamut of life, a range of appeal wider than the gardens; the impunities of lawless Nature reach farther than man's finished strokes. Nay, when man has done his best in a garden, some shall even regret, for sentimental reasons, that he brought Art upon the scene at all. "Even after the wild landscape, through which youth had strayed at will, has been laid out into fields and gardens, and enclosed with fences and hedges; after the footsteps, which had bounded over the flower-strewn grass have been circumscribed within firm gravel-walks, the vision of its former happiness will still at times float before the mind in its dreams." ("Guesses at Truth.")

Beauty, Romance, and Nature await an audience with you in the garden; but it is Beauty after she has been sent to school to learn the tricks of conscious grace; Beauty that has "the foreign aid of ornament," that walks with the supple gait of one who has been well drilled; but gone are the fine careless raptures, gone the bounding step, the blithe impulses of unschooled freedom and gipsy life out of doors.

Romance awaits you, holding in her hand a picture of things bright and jocund, full of tender colour and sweet suggestion; a picture designed to prove this world to be unruffled Arcadia, a sunlit pageant, a dream of delectation, a place for solace, a Herrick-land

"Of brooks, of blossoms, birds, and bowers;"

and human life a jewelled tale with all the irony left out.

Nature awaits you, but only as a fair captive, ready to respond to your behests, to answer to the spring of your imaginings. To man's wooing, "I love you, love me back," she resigned herself, not perceiving the drift of homage that was paid not so much to the beauty that she had, but to the beauty of a heightened sort that should ensue upon his cultivation, for the sake of which he sought her. So now her wildness is subdued. The yew and the holly from the tangled brake shall feel the ignominy of the shears. The "common" thorn of the hedge shall be grafted with one of the twenty-seven rarer sorts; the oak and maple shall be headed down and converted into scarlet species; the single flowers, obedient to a beautiful disease, shall blow as doubles, and be propagated by scientific processes that defy Nature and accomplish centuries of evolution at a stride. The woodbine from the vernal wood must be nailed to the carpenter's trellis, the brook may no more brawl, nor violate its limits, the leaves of the hollybush and the box shall be variegated, the forest tree and woodland shrub shall have their frayed hedges shorn, and their wildness pressed out of them in Art's dissembling embrace.

And as with the green things of the earth, so with the creatures of the animal world that are admitted into the sanctuary of a garden. Here is no place for nonconformity of any kind. True, the spruce little squirrel asks no leave for his dashing raids upon the beech-mast and the sweet chestnuts that have escaped the range of the gardener's broom; true, the white and golden pheasant and the speckled goligny may moon about in their distraught fashion down the green alleys and in and out the shrubberies; the foreign duck may frisk in the lake; the white swan may hoist her sail, and "float double, swan and shadow;" the birds may sing in the trees; the peacock may strut on the lawn, or preen his feathers upon

ON THE OTHER SIDE.—A PLEA FOR SAVAGERY. 191

the terrace walls; the fallow deer may browse among the bracken on the other side of the ha-ha—thus much of the animal creation shall be allowed here, and not the most fastidious son of Adam will protest a word. But note the terms of their admission. They are a select company, gathered with nice judgment from all quarters of the globe, that are bound over to respectable behaviour, pledged to the beautiful or picturesque; they are in chains, though the chains be aerial and not seen.

It is not that the gardener loves pheasants or peacocks, ducks or swans or guinea-fowls for themselves, or for their contribution to the music of the place. Not this, but because these creatures assist the garden's magic, they support the illusion upon which the whole thing is based; as they flit about, and cross and recross the scene, and scream, and quack, and cackle, you get a touch of actuality that adds finish to the strangeness and piquancy that prevail around; they verify your doubting vision, and make valid the reality of its ideality; they accord with the well-swept lawn, the scented air, the flashing radiance of the fountain, the white statuary backed by dark yews or dim stone alcoves, with the clipt shrubs, the dreaming trees, the blare of bright colours, in the shapely beds, the fragrant odours and select beauties of the place. These living creatures (for they *are* alive), prowling about the grounds,* looking fairly comfortable in artificial

---

* Lord Beaconsfield adds macaws to the ornament of his ideal garden. "Sir Ferdinand, when he resided at Armine, was accustomed

surroundings from whence their clipped wings will not allow them to escape, incline you to believe that this world is a smooth, genteel, beneficent world after all, and its pastoral character is here so well sustained that no one would be a bit surprised if Pan with his pipe of reeds, or Corydon with his white-fleeced flock, should turn the corner at any moment.

It is only upon man's terms, however, and to suit his scheme of scenic effects, that these tame things are allowed on the premises. They are not here because man loves them. Woe to the satin-coated mole that blindly burrows on the lawn! Woe to the rabbit that sneaks through the fence, or to the hare that leaps it! Woe to the red fox that litters in the pinetum, or to the birds that make nests in the shrubberies! Woe to the otter that takes license to fish in the ponds at the bottom of the pleasaunce! Woe to the blackbirds that strip the rowan-tree of its berries just when autumn visitors are expected! Woe to the finches that nip the buds off the fruit-trees in the hard spring frost, presuming upon David's plea for sacrilege! Death, instant or prolonged, or dear life purchased at the price of a torn limb, for the silly things that dare to stray where the woodland liberties are forbidden to either plant or animal!

to fill these pleasure grounds with macaws and other birds of gorgeous plumage." But Lord Beaconsfield is Benjamin Disraeli—a master of the ornate, a bit of a dandy always. In Italy, too, they throw in porcupines and ferrets for picturesqueness. In Holland are our old friends the tin hare and guinea-pigs, and the happy shooting boy, in holiday attire, painted to the life.

So much for the results of man's manipulation of the universe in the way of making ornamental grounds! And the sketch here given applies equally to the new style or to the old, to the garden after Loudon or to the garden after Bacon; the destiny of things is equally interfered with to meet the requirements of the one or the other; the styles are equally artificial, equally remorseless to primal Nature.

But one may go farther, and ask: What wonder at the outcry of the modern Nature-lovers against a world so altered from its original self as that Hawthorne should say of England in general that here "the wildest things are more than half tame? The trees, for instance, whether in hedgerow, park, or what they call forest, have nothing wild about them. They are never ragged; there is a certain decorous restraint in the freest outspread of their branches!" Nay, so far does this mistaken man carry his diseased appetite for English soil, marred as it is, that he shall write: "To us Americans there is a kind of sanctity even in an English turnip-field, when we think how long that small square of ground has been known and recognised as a possession, transmitted from father to son, trodden often by memorable feet, and utterly redeemed from savagery by old acquaintance with civilised eyes" ("Our Old Home," p. 75).

What wonder, I say, that a land that is so hopelessly gardened as this—a land so sentimentalised and humanised that its very clods, to the American,

o

are "poesy all ramm'd with life"—shall grate the nerves of the Hamlets of to-day, who live too much in the sun, whom man delights not, nor woman neither!

What a land to live in! when its best landscape painters—men like Gainsborough or Constable—are so carried away by the influence of agriculture upon landscape, so lost to the superiority of wild solitude, that they will plainly tell you that they like the fields the farmers work in, and the work they do in them; preferring Nature that was modified by man, painting a well-cultivated country with villages and mills and church-steeples seen over hedges and between trees!*

What a land to live in! when even Nature's wild children of field and forest hug their chains—preserve their old ways and habits up to the very frontier-line of civilisation. For here is Jefferies (who ought to know) writing thus: "Modern progress, except where it has exterminated them, has scarcely touched the habits of bird or animal; so almost up to the very houses of the metropolis the nightingale yearly returns to her old haunts. If we go a few hours' journey only, and then step just beyond the highway, where the steam ploughing-engine has left the mark of its wide wheels on the dust, and glance into the hedgerow, the copse, or stream, there are Nature's children as unrestrained in their wild, free life as they were in the veritable backwoods of primitive England."

* See P. G Hamerton's "Sylvan Year," p. 112.

What wonder that a land where Nature has thus succumbed wholesale to culture, should exasperate the man who has earned a right to be morbid, or that he should cry aloud in his despair, "I am tired of civilised Europe, and I want to see a *wild* country if I can." Too many are our spots renowned for beauty, our smiling champaigns of flower and fruit. For "Fair prospects wed happily with fair times; but, alas, if times be not fair!" Hence the comfort of oppressive surroundings over-sadly tinged, to men who suffer from the mockery of a place that is too smiling! Hence the glory of a waste like Egdon to Mr. Hardy! ("The Return of the Native," pp. 4, 5). For Egdon Heath, "Haggard Egdon appealed to a subtler and scarcer instinct, to a more recently learnt emotion than that which responds to the sort of beauty called charming and fair. Indeed, it is a question if the exclusive reign of this orthodox beauty is not approaching its last quarter. The new Vale of Tempe may be a gaunt waste in Thule; human souls may find themselves in closer and closer harmony with external things wearing a sombreness distasteful to our race when it was young. The time seems near, if it has not acutally arrived, when the chastened sublimity of a moor, a sea, or a mountain will be all of Nature that is absolutely in keeping with the moods of the more thinking of mankind. And ultimately, to the commonest tourist, spots like Iceland may become what the vineyards and myrtle-gardens of South Europe are to him now; and Heidelberg and Baden be passed unheeded as he hastens from the Alps to the sand-dunes of Scheveningen."

I admit that it is strange that time should hold in reserve such revenges as this ascetic writing denotes—strange that man should find beauty irksome, and that he should feel blasted with the very ecstasy himself has built up in a garden! strange this sudden recoil of the smooth son of culture from the extreme of Art, to the extreme of Nature! Stranger still that the "Yes" and "No" of the *Ideal* Hyde and the *Real* Jekyll should consist in the same bosom, and that a man shall be, as it were, a prey to contrary maladies at one and the same time! Yet we have found this in Bacon—prince of fine gardeners, who with all his seeming content with the heroic pleasaunce that he has made, shall still betray a sneaking fondness for the maiden charms of Bohemia outside. Earthly Paradise is fine and fit, but there must needs be "mounts of some pretty height, leaving the wall of the enclosure breast high to look abroad in the fields"—there must be "a window open, to fly out at, a secret way to retire by." Nay, after all, what are to him the charms that inspire his rhapsody of words—the things that princes add for state and magnificence! They are Delilah's charms, and "but nothing to the true pleasure of a garden!"

"Our gardens in Paris," says Joubert, "smell musty; I do not like these ever-green trees. There is something of blackness in their greenery, of coldness in their shade. Besides, since they neither lose anything, nor have anything to fear, they seem to me unfeeling, and hence have little interest for me. . . . Those irregular gardens, which we call English gardens, require a labyrinth for a dwelling."

"I hate those trees that never lose their foliage" (says Landor); "they seem to have no sympathy with Nature; winter and summer are alike to them." Says Thomson,

> ". . . . . "For loveliness
> Needs not the foreign aid of ornament,
> But it is when unadorned adorn'd the most."

Or Cowley's

> "My garden painted o'er
> With Nature's hand, not Art's; and pleasures yield,
> Horace might envy in his Sabine field."

Or Addison: "I have often looked upon it as a piece of happiness that I have never fallen into any of these fantastical tastes, nor esteemed anything the more for its being uncommon and hard to be met with. For this reason I look upon the whole country in spring-time as a spacious garden, and make as many visits to a spot of daisies, or a bank of violets, as a florist does to his borders or parterres. There is not a bush in blossom within a mile of me which I am not acquainted with, nor scarce a daffodil or cowslip that withers away in my neighbourhood without my missing it." Or Rousseau: "I can imagine, said I to them, a rich man from Paris or London, who should be master of this house, bringing with him an expensive architect to spoil Nature. With what disdain would he enter this simple and mean place! With what contempt would he have all these tatters uprooted! What fine avenues he would open out! What beautiful alleys he would have pierced! What fine goose-feet, what fine trees like parasols and fans! What finely fretted trellises! What beautifully-drawn yew hedges, finely squared and rounded! What fine bowling-greens of fine English turf, rounded, squared, sloped, ovaled; what fine yews carved into dragons, pagodas, marmosets, every kind of monster! With what fine bronze vases, what fine stone-founts he would adorn his garden! When all that is carried out, said M. De Wolmar, he will have made a very fine place, which one will scarcely enter, and will always be anxious to leave to seek the country."

Or Gautier, upon Nature's wild growths: "You will find in her domain a thousand exquisitely pretty little corners into which man seldom or never penetrates. There, from every constraint, she gives herself up to that delightful extravagance of dishevelled plants, of glowing flowers and wild vegetation—everything that germinates, flowers, and casts its seeds, instinct with an eager vitality, to the wind, whose mission it is to disperse them broadcast with an unsparing hand. . . . And over the rain-washed gate, bare of paint, and having no trace of that green colour beloved by Rousseau, we should have written this inscription in black letters, stone-like in shape, and threatening in aspect:

'GARDENERS ARE PROHIBITED FROM ENTERING HERE.'

"Such a whim—very difficult for one to realise who is so deeply incrusted with civilisation, where the least originality is taxed as folly—is continually indulged in by Nature, who laughs at the judgment of fools."

Or Thoreau—hero of the Walden shanty, with his open-air gospel—all Nature for the asking—to whom a garden is but Nature debauched, and all Art a sin: "There is in my nature, methinks, a singular yearning towards wildness. . . . We are apt enough to be pleased with such books as Evelyn's 'Sylva,' 'Acetarium,' and 'Kalendarium Hortense,' but they imply a relaxed nerve in the reader. Gardening is civil and social, but it wants the vigour and freedom of the forest and the outlaw. . . . It is true there are the innocent pleasures of country-life, and it is sometimes pleasant to make the earth yield her increase, and gather the fruits in their season, but the heroic spirit will not fail to dream of remoter retirements and more rugged paths. It will have its garden-plots and its *parterres* elsewhere than on the earth, and gather nuts and berries by the way for its subsistence, or orchard fruits with such heedlessness as berries. We should not be always soothing and training Nature. . . . The Indian's intercourse with Nature is at least such as admits of the greatest independence of each. If he is somewhat of a stranger in her midst, the gardener is too much of a familiar. There is something vulgar and foul in the latter's closeness to his mistress, something noble and cleanly in the former's distance. . .

There are other savager, and more primeval aspects of Nature than our poets have sung. It is only white man's poetry."

To sum up the whole matter, this unmitigated hostility of the cultured man (with Jacob's smooth hands and Esau's wild blood) to the amenities of civilised life, brings us back to the point from whence we started at the commencement of this chapter. While men are what they are, Art is not all. Man has Viking passions as well as Eden instincts. <u>Man is of mixed blood, whose sympathies are not so much divided as double.</u> And all of man asks for all of Nature, and is not content with less. To the over-civilised man who is under a cloud, the old contentment with orthodox beauty must give place to the subtler, scarcer instinct, to "the more recently learnt emotion, than that which responds to the sort of beauty called charming and fair." Fair effects are only for fair times. The garden represents to such an one a too careful abstract of Nature's traits and features that had better not have been epitomised. The place is to him a kind of fraud—a forgery, so to speak, of Nature's autograph. It is only the result of man's turning spy or detective upon the beauties of the outer world. Its perfection is too monotonous; its grace is too subtle; its geography too bounded; its interest too full of intention—too much sharpened to a point; its growth is too uniformly temperate; its imagery too exacting of notice. These prim and trim things remind him of captive princes of the wood, brightly attired only that they may give romantic interest to the garden—these tame birds with clipped wings, of distraught aspect and dreamy tread—these docile animals with their limp legs and vacant stare, may contribute to the scenic pomp of the place, but it is at the expense of their native instincts and the joyous *abandon* of woodland life. If this be the outcome of your boasted editing of Nature, give us dead Nature untranslated. If this be what comes of your idealisation of the raw materials of Nature—of the transference of your own emotions to the simple, unsophisticated things of the common earth, let us rather have Nature's unspoilt self—" God's Art," as Plato calls Nature—where

> "Visions, as prophetic eyes avow,
> Hang on each leaf, and cling to each bough."

"But stay, here come the gardeners!"
(*Enter a gardener and two servants.*)—*King Richard II.*

CHAPTER IX.

IN PRAISE OF BOTH.

"In small proportions we just beauties see,
  And in short measures life may perfect be."—BEN JONSON.

"The Common all men have."—GEORGE HERBERT.

WHAT shall we say, then, to the two conflicting views of garden-craft referred to in my last chapter, wherein I take the modern position, namely, that the love of Art in a garden, and the love of wild things in Nature's large estate, cannot co-exist in the same breast? Is the position true or false?

To see the matter in its full bearings I must fetch back a little, and recall what was said in a former chapter (p. 85) upon the differing attitudes towards Nature taken by the earlier and later schools of gardening. There is, I said, no trace in the writings, or in the gardening, of the earlier traditional school, of that mawkish sentiment about Nature, that condescending tenderness for her primal shapes, that has nursed the scruples, and embarrassed the efforts of the "landscape-gardener" from Kent's and Brown's days to now.

The older gardener had no half-and-half methods; he made no pretence of Nature-worship, nursed no scruples that could hinder the expression of his own mind about Nature, or check him from fathoming all her possibilities. Yet with all his seeming unscrupulousness the old gardener does not close his eyes or his heart to Nature at large, but whether in the garden sanctuary or out of it, he maintains equally tender relations towards her.

But the scruples of the earlier phase of the landscape school, about tampering with Nature by way of attaining Art effects, are as water unto wine compared with what is taught by men of the same school now-a-days. We have now to reckon with an altogether deeper stratum of antipathy to garden-craft than was reached by the followers of Brown. We have not now to haggle with the quidnuncs over the less or more of Art permissible in a garden, but to fight out the question whether civilisation shall have any garden at all. Away with this "white man's poetry!" The wild Indian's "intercourse with Nature is at least such as admits of the greatest independence of each. If he is somewhat of a stranger in her midst, the gardener is too much of a familiar. There is something vulgar and foul in the latter's closeness to his mistress, something noble and cleanly in the former's distance." "Alas!" says Newman, "what are we doing all through life, both as a necessity and a duty, but unlearning the world's poetry, and attaining to its prose?"

One does not fear, however, that the English people will part lightly with their land's old poetry, however seductive the emotion which we are told "prefers the oppression of surroundings over-sadly tinged, and solitudes that have a lonely face, suggesting tragical possibilities to the old-fashioned sort of beauty called charming and fair."

The lesson we have to learn is the falsehood of extremes. The point we have to master is, that in the prodigality of "God's Plenty" many sorts of beauty are ours, and nothing shall be scorned. God's creation has a broad gamut, a vast range, to meet our many moods. "There are, it may be, so many kinds of music in the world, and none of them is without signification."

"O world, as God has made it! All is beauty."

There is nothing contradictory in the variety and multiformity of Nature, whether loose and at large in Nature's unmapped geography, or garnered and assorted and heightened by man's artistry in the small proportions of a perfect garden. Man, we said, is of mixed blood, whose sympathies are not so much divided as double, and each sympathy shall have free play. My inborn Eden instincts draw me to the bloom and wonder of the world; my Viking blood drives me to the snap and enthusiasm of anarchic forms, the colossal images, the swarthy monotony, the sombre aspects of Nature in the wild. Yet "all is beauty."

Thus much by way of preamble. And now, after repeating that the gardener of the old formality, however sternly he discipline wild Nature for the purposes of beauty, is none the less capable of loving and of holding friendly commerce with the things that grew outside his garden hedge, let me bring upon my page a modern of moderns, who, by the wide range of his sympathies, recalls the giants of a healthier day, and redeems a generation of lop-sided folk abnormally developed in one direction.

And the poet Wordsworth, self-drawn in his own works, or depicted by his friends, is one of the old stock of sane, sound-hearted Englishmen, who can be equally susceptible to the *inward* beauties of man's created brain-world, and the *outward* beauties of unkempt Nature. So the combination we plead for is not impossible! The two tastes are not irreconcilable! Blessed be both!

We may trust Wordsworth implicitly as an authority upon Nature. No one questions his knowledge of wild woodland lore. There is no one of ancient or of modern times who in his outward mien, his words, his habits, carries more indisputable proof of the prophet's ordination than the man who spent a long noviciate in his native mountain solitudes. There is no one so fully entitled, or so well able to speak of and for her, as he who knows her language to the faintest whisper, who spent his days at her feet, who pored over her lineaments under every change of expression, who in his writings drew upon the secret honey of the beauty and harmony of the world, telling, to use his own swinging phrases, of "the joy and happiness of loving creatures, of men and children, of birds and beasts, of hills and streams, and trees and flowers; with the changes of night and day, evening and morning, summer and winter; and all their unwearied actions and energies."

Of all Nature's consecrated children, he is the prince of the apostolate; he is, so to speak, the beloved disciple of them all, whose exalted personal love admits him to the right to lean upon her breast, to hear her heart-beats, to catch knowledge there that had been kept secret since the world began. None so familiar with pastoral life in its varied timefulness, sweet or stern, glad or grim, pathetic or sublime, as he who carries in his mind the echoes of the passion of the storm, the moan of the passing wind with its beat upon the bald mountain-crag, the sighing of the dry sedge, the lunge of mighty waters, the tones of water-falls, the inland sounds of caves and trees, the plaintive spirit of the solitude. There are none who have pondered so deeply over "the blended holiness of earth and sky," the gesture of the wind and cloud, the silence of the hills; none so free to fraternise with things bold or obscure, great or small, as he who told alike of the love and infinite longings of Margaret, of the fresh joy of

> "The blooming girl whose hair was wet
> With points of morning dew,"

of the lonely star, the solitary raven, the pliant hare-bell, swinging in the breeze, the meadows and the lower ground, and all the sweetness of a common dawn.

Thus did Wordsworth enter into the soul of things and sing of them

> "In a music sweeter than their own."

Nay, says Arnold, "It might seem that Nature not only gave him the matter of his poem, but wrote his poem for him" ("Essays in Criticism," p. 155).

So much for Wordsworth upon Nature out of doors; now let us hear him upon Art in a garden, of which he was fully entitled to speak, and we shall see that the man is no less the poet of idealism upon his own ground, than the poet of actuality in the woodland world.

Writing to his friend Sir Geo. Beaumont,* with all the outspokenness of friendship and the simplicity of a candid mind, he thus delivers himself upon the Art of Gardening: "Laying out grounds, as it is called, may be considered as a liberal Art, in some sort like poetry and painting, and its object is, or ought to be, to move the affections under the control of good sense; that is, those of the best and wisest; but, *speaking with more precision, it is to assist Nature in moving the affections of those who have the deepest perception of the beauties of Nature, who have the most valuable feelings, that is, the most permanent, the most independent, the most ennobling with Nature and human life.*"

Hearken to Nature's own high priest, turned laureate of the garden! How can this thing be? Here is the man whose days had been spent at Nature's feet, whose life's business seemed to be this only, that he should extol her, interpret her, sing of her, lift her as high in man's esteem as fine utterance can affect the human soul. Yet when he has

---

* See Myers' "Wordsworth," English Men of Letters Series, p. 67.

done all, said all that inspired imagination can say in her praise, in what seems an outburst of disloyalty to his old mistress, he deliberately takes the crown himself had woven from off the head of Nature and places it on the brows of Art in a garden!

Not Bacon himself could write with more discernment or with more fervour of garden-craft than this, and the pronouncement gains further significance as being the deliberately expressed opinion of a great poet, and him the leader of the modern School of Naturalists. And that these two men, separated not merely by two centuries of time, but by the revolutionary influences which coloured them, should find common ground and shake hands in a garden, is strange indeed! Both men loved Nature. Bacon, as Dean Church remarks,* had a "keen delight in Nature, in the beauty and scents of flowers, in the charm of open-air life;" but his regard for Nature's beauties was not so ardent, his knowledge of her works and ways not so intimate or so scientifically verified, his senses not so sympathetically allured as Wordsworth's; he had not the same prophet's vision that could see into the life of things, and find thoughts there "that do often lie too deep for tears." That special sense Wordsworth himself fathered.

Points like these add weight to Wordsworth's testimony of the high rank of gardening, and we do well to note that the wreath that the modern man brings for Art in a garden is not only greener and

---

* "Bacon," English Men of Letters Series, R. W. Church.

fresher than the garland of the other, but it was gathered on loftier heights; it means more, it implies a more emphatic homage.

And Wordsworth had not that superficial knowledge of gardening which no gentleman's head should be without. He knew it as a craftsman knows the niceties of his craft. "More than one seat in the lake-country," says Mr. Myers ("Wordsworth," p. 68), "among them one home of pre-eminent beauty, have owed to Wordsworth no small part of their ordered charm."

Of Wordsworth's own garden, one writes: "I know that thirty years ago that which struck me most at Rydal Mount, and which appeared to me its greatest charm, was the union of the garden and the wilderness. You passed almost imperceptibly from the trim parterre to the noble wood, and from the narrow, green vista to that wide sweep of lake and mountain which made up one of the finest landscapes in England. Nor could you doubt that this unusual combination was largely the result of the poet's own care and arrangement. *He had the faculty for such work.*"

Here one may well leave the matter without further labouring, content to have proved by the example of a four-square, sane genius, that those instincts of ours which seem to pull contrary ways—Art-wards or Nature-wards—and to drive our lop-sided selves to the falsehood of extremes, are, after all, not incompatible. The field, the waste, the moor, the mountain, the trim garden with its parterres and terraces, are one Nature. These things breathe one breath, they sing one music, they share one heart between them; the difference between the dressed and the undressed is only superficial. The art of gardening is not intended to supersede Nature, but only " to assist Nature in moving the affections of those who have the deepest perceptions of the beauties of Nature, who have the most valuable feelings, . . the most ennobling with Nature and human life."

One need not, if Wordsworth's example prove anything, be less the child of the present (but rather the more) because one can both appreciate the realities of rude Nature, and that deliberately-contrived, purpose-made, piece of human handicraft, a well-equipped garden. One need not be less susceptible to the black forebodings of this contention-tost, modern world, nor need one's ear be less alert to Nature's correspondence to

"The still, sad music of humanity,"

because one experiences with old Mountaine, "a jucunditie of minde" in a fair garden. There is an unerring rightness both in rude Nature and in garden grace, in the chartered liberty of the one, and the unchartered freedom of unadjusted things in the other. Blessed be both!

It is worth something to have mastered truth, which, however simple and elementary it seem, is really vital to the proper understanding of the relation of Art to Nature. It helps one to appraise at their proper value the denunciations of the disciples of

Kent and Brown against Art in a garden, and to see, on the other hand, why Bacon and the Early School of gardeners loved Nature in the wild state no less than in a garden. It dispels any lingering hesitation we may have as to the amount of Art a garden may receive in defiance of Dryasdust "codes of taste." It explains what your artist-gardener friend meant when he said that he had as much sympathy with, and felt as much interest in, the moving drama of Nature going on on this as on that side of his garden-hedge, and how he could pass from the rough theme outside to the ordered music inside, from the uncertain windings in the coppice-glade to the pleached alley of the garden, without sense of disparagement to the one or the other. It explains why it is that nothing in Nature goes unobserved of him; how you shall call to see him and hunt the garden over, and at last find him idling along the bridle-path in the plantation, his fist full of flowers, his mind set on Nature's affairs, his ear in such unison with local sounds that he shall tell you the dominant tone of the wind in the tree-tops. Or he is in the covert's tangle enjoying

"Simple Nature's breathing life,"

surprising the thorn veiled in blossom, revelling in the wealth of boundless life there, in the variety of plant-form, the palpitating lights, the melody of nesting birds, the common joy and sweet assurance of things.

"Society is all but rude
To this delicious solitude."

Or it may be he is on the breezy waste, lying full length among the heather, watching the rabbits' gambols, or the floating thistle-down with its hint of unseen life in the air, or sauntering by the stream in the lower meadows, learning afresh the glory of weed life in the lush magnificence of the great docks, the red sorrel, the willow-herb, the purple thistles, and the gay battalions of fox-gloves thrown out in skirmishing order, that swarm on each eminence and hedgerow. Or you may meet him hastening home for the evening view from the orchard-terrace, to see the solemn close of day, and the last gleam of sunshine fading over the hill.

It is worth something, I say, to win clear hold of the fact that Nature in a garden and Nature in the wild are at unity; that they have each their place in the economy of human life, and that each should have its share in man's affections. The true gardener is in touch with both. He knows where this excels or fails behind the other, and because he knows the range of each, he fears no comparison between them. He can be eloquent upon the charms of a garden, its stimulus for the tired eye and mind, the harmony that resides in the proportions of its lines and masses, the gladness of its colour, the delight of its frankly decorative arrangement, the sense of rest that comes of its symmetry and repeated patterns. He will tell you that for halcyon days, when life's wheels run smooth, and the sun shines, even for life's average days, there is nothing so cheery, nothing so blithely companionable, nothing that can give such a sense of household warmth to your home as a pleasant garden. And yet none will be more ready to warn you of the <u>limits of a garden's charms, of its sheer impotence to yield satisfaction at either end of the scale of human joy or sorrow.</u>

And so it is. Let but the mist of melancholy descend upon you, let but the pessimistic distress to which we moderns are all prone penetrate your mind, let you be the prey of undermining sorrow, or lie under the shadow of bereavement, and it is not to the garden that you will go for Nature's comfort. The chalices of its flowers store not the dew that shall cool your brow. Nay, at times like these the garden poses as a kind of lovely foe, to mock you with its polite reticence, its look of unwavering complacency, its gentle ecstasy. Then the ear refuses the soft and intimate garden-melodies, and asks instead for the rough unrehearsed music of Nature in the wild, the jar and jangle of winds and tides, the challenge of discords,

"The conflict and the sounds that live in darkness,"

the wild rhetoric of the night upon some "haggard Egdon," or along the steep wild cliffs when the storm is up, and the deeps are troubled, and the earth throbs and throbs again with the violence of the waves that break and bellow in the caves beneath your feet; and then it perhaps shall cross your mind to set this brief moment of your despair against the unavailing passion of tides that for ten thousand years and more have hurled themselves against this heedless shore. Or you shall find some sequestered corner of the land that keeps its scars of old-world turmoil, the symptoms of the hustle of primeval days, the shock of grim shapes, long ago put to sleep beneath a coverlet of sweet-scented turf; and the unspoiled grandeur of the scene will prick and arouse your dulled senses, while its peaceful face will assure you that, as it was with the troubled masonry of the hills in the morning of the world, even so shall it be with you—time shall tranquillise and at length cancel all your woes. Or again,

> "Should life be dull, and spirits low
> 'Twill soothe us in our sorrow
> That earth has something yet to show,
> The bonny holms of Yarrow."

Better tonic, one thinks, for the over-wrought brain than the soft glamour of the well-swept lawn, the clipt shrubs, the focussed beauty of dotted specimens, the ordered disorder of wriggling paths and sprawling flower-beds of strange device, the ransacked wardrobe of the gardener's stock of gay bedding-plants, or other of the permitted charms of a modern garden; better than these is the stir and enthusiasm of Nature's broad estate, the boulder-tossed moor, where the hare runs races in her mirth, and the lark has a special song for your ear; or the high transport of hours of indolence spent basking in the bed of purple heather, your nostrils filled with gladsome air and the scent of thyme, your eyes following the course of the milk-white clouds that ride with folded sails in the blue heavens overhead and cast flying shadows on the uplands, where nothing breaks the silence of the hills but the song in the air, the tinkle of the sheep-bells, and the murmur of the moorland bee.

And the upshot of the matter is this. The master-things for the enjoyment of life are: health, a balanced mind that will not churlishly refuse "God's plenty," an eye quick to discern the marvel of beautiful things, a heart in sympathy with man and beast. Possessing these we may defy Fortune—

> " I care not, Fortune, what you me deny:
> You cannot rob me of free Nature's grace,
> You cannot shut the windows of the sky
> Through which Aurora shows her brightening face ;
> You cannot bar my constant feet to trace
> The woods and lawns, by living stream, at eve :
> Let health my nerves and finer fibres brace,
> And I their toys to the great children leave ;
> Of fancy, reason, virtue, nought can me bereave."

PRINTED BY
THE HANSARD PUBLISHING UNION, LIMITED, LONDON
AND REDHILL.

www.ingramcontent.com/pod-product-compliance
Lightning Source LLC
Chambersburg PA
CBHW031956230426
43672CB00010B/2170